Double Dialectics

Double Dialectics

Between Universalism and Relativism in Enlightenment and Postmodern Thought

CLAUDIA MOSCOVICI

ROWMAN & LITTLEFIELD PUBLISHERS, INC.
Lanham • Boulder • New York • Oxford

ROWMAN & LITTLEFIELD PUBLISHERS, INC.

Published in the United States of America
by Rowman & Littlefield Publishers, Inc.
4720 Boston Way, Lanham, Maryland 20706
www.rowmanlittlefield.com

12 Hid's Copse Road
Cumnor Hill, Oxford OX2 9JJ, England

Copyright © 2002 by Rowman & Littlefield Publishers, Inc.

All rights reserved. No part of this publication may be reproduced, stored in a retrieval system, or transmitted in any form or by any means, electronic, mechanical, photocopying, recording, or otherwise, without the prior permission of the publisher.

British Library Cataloguing in Publication Information Available

Library of Congress Cataloging-in-Publication Data

Moscovici, Claudia, 1969–
   Double dialectics : between universalism and relativism in Enlightenment and postmodern thought / Claudia Moscovici.
     p. cm.
   Includes bibliographical references and index.
   ISBN 0-7425-1368-8 (alk. paper)
   1. Postmodernism. 2. Enlightenment. 3. Universals (Philosophy) 4. Relativity. 5. Knowledge, Theory of. 6. Ethics, Modern. I. Title

B831.2 M675 2002
190—dc21

2001048

Printed in the United States of America

∞™ The paper used in this publication meets the minimum requirements of American National Standard for Information Sciences—Permanence of Paper for Printed Library Materials, ANSI/NISO Z39.48-1992.

Contents

Acknowledgments   vii

Introduction
Between Universalism and Relativism:
Philosophizing Common Sense   1

Chapter One
The Postmodern Need for a Philosophy of
Common Sense: Lyotard's *The Postmodern
Condition* and *The Differend*   13

Chapter Two
Dialectical Deduction: A Reading of Kant's
Critique of Pure Reason   29

Chapter Three
Beyond the Particular and the Universal:
D'Alembert's "Discours préliminaire" to
the *Encyclopédie*   51

Chapter Four
An Ethics of Cultural Exchange: Diderot's
Supplément au Voyage de Bougainville   75

CONTENTS

Chapter Five
Hybridity and Ethics in Chateaubriand's *Atala* 93

Chapter Six
The Dialectical Process of Decolonialization:
Fanon's *The Wretched of the Earth* 113

Chapter Seven
The Problem of Cultural Relativism: Said's
Orientalism and *The World, the Text, and the Critic* 129

Bibliography 157

Index 163

About the Author 169

Acknowledgments

The idea for this book originated from the exchanges I had with Daniel Brewer on a panel on Enlightenment encyclopedias organized by Julie Hayes at the American Society for Eighteenth-Century Studies convention in 1997. I would like to thank both of them for their input and ideas during that discussion. I would also like to thank Nancy Armstrong for her critical reading of the chapter on d'Alembert's "Discours préliminaire" to the *Encyclopédie*. Likewise, I am grateful to Marshall Olds for his encouraging words regarding the chapter on Chateaubriand's *Atala*.

A version of the chapter "Beyond the Particular and the Universal: D'Alembert's 'Discours préliminaire' to the *Encyclopédie*" appeared in *Eighteenth-Century Studies*, vol. 33, no. 3 (2000) and in *Perusals into Postmodern Thought* (University Press of America, 2000). A version of the chapter "The Postmodern Need for a Philosophy of Common Sense: Lyotard's *The Postmodern Condition* and *The Differend*" also appeared in *Perusals into Postmodern Thought*. The chapter "Hybridity and Ethics in Chateaubriand's *Atala*" appeared as an article in *Nineteenth-Century French Studies* (Spring–Summer 2001).

I am deeply indebted to the general support of my family and friends. I would like to express special thanks to my friends and colleagues, Nelly Furman, Mary Harper, Shen Lin Hu, Pascal Ifri, John Isbell, Tom Kavanagh, Dottie Kelly, Natalie McKnight, Catherine Perry, Antoinette Sol, Allen Thiher, Lesley Walker, and Henry Wend for their support.

ACKNOWLEDGMENTS

To my family I owe much of the energy and impetus to write. I particularly wish to thank my husband, Dan Troyka, for his significant input on the chapter on Kant's epistemology and, more generally, for his love and support throughout our ten years of marriage.

INTRODUCTION

Between Universalism and Relativism: Philosophizing Common Sense

The intellectual debates of two hundred years ago continue to engage scholars today. Enlightenment philosophers, including David Hume, George Berkeley, Immanuel Kant, Jean Le Rond d'Alembert and Denis Diderot, addressed fundamental questions such as: What is the nature of human knowledge? Can we know reality in itself, or is knowledge limited by our personal and human perspective? What is the basis of moral conduct? Are there any universal moral guidelines that should be followed by all human beings, or is ethics a matter of custom and even subjective opinion? Enlightenment thinkers offered vastly different responses to these questions. Hume famously undermined the certainty of knowledge; Berkeley posited that knowledge was the product of thought; while Kant and d'Alembert charted different paths between truth and doubt. Despite their unique responses, however, Enlightenment philosophers shared some common assumptions. For them, speculation about the basis and purpose of human existence was a worthwhile endeavor that advanced not only scholarly work, but also human thought in general. They also believed that philosophical discourse had to provide new and undogmatic answers to age-old metaphysical questions. Kant, for instance, maintained that one of the main goals of his critique of reason was to combat the widely shared assumption that knowledge is objectively true if it is a product of rational thought. In the *Prolegomena to Any Future Metaphysics*,[1] which elucidated the main arguments of the *Critique of Pure Reason*,[2] he declared:

> Weary therefore of dogmatism, which teaches us nothing, and of skepticism, which does not even promise us anything, not even to rest in permitted

ignorance; disquieted by the importance of knowledge so much needed; and, lastly, rendered suspicious by long experience of all knowledge which we believe we possess or which offers itself under the title of pure reason—we have left but one critical question upon whose answer depends our future conduct, viz., is metaphysics itself possible? (21)

Contemporary postmodernists claim to answer Kant's question by turning not only the question, but also the foundation of Enlightenment thought, on its head. According to postmodern critics such as Lyotard, the main question is not whether inquiries into the nature of reality are possible, but what are the effects of such futile pursuits. Sounding like Kant but undoing his philosophical project, Lyotard advises readers against accepting the concepts of reality, truth, and morality. Philosophical discourses, Lyotard declares in *The Postmodern Condition*,[3] consist of nothing but powerful stories, or "metanarratives," that have sedimented over time and that we accept unthinkingly and defend dogmatically. To enter the postmodern era, he suggests, we must overcome our Enlightenment legacy by abandoning the quest for truth:

> I will use the term *modern* to designate any science that legitimates itself with reference to a metadiscourse of this kind by making an explicit appeal to some grand narrative, such as the dialectics of Spirit, the hermeneutics of meaning, the emancipation of the rational or working subject or the creation of wealth. For example, the rule of consensus between sender and addressee of a statement with truth-value is deemed acceptable if it is cast in terms of a possible unanimity between rational minds: this is the Enlightenment narrative, in which the hero of knowledge works toward a good ethico-political end—universal peace. (xxiii)

Lyotard groups together Enlightenment and contemporary universalist theories. Placing Kant and Habermas in the same boat, he argues that universalist philosophy pursues what I will describe as a single dialectical logic that aims to eliminate multiplicity and heterogeneity. Only by suppressing (or negating) difference, Lyotard suggests, can universalist philosophers create a (false) sense of shared moral norms and epistemological standards. Having defined modern discourse as unitary, Lyotard pursues an inverse dialectical process to define postmodernism:

> Simplifying to the extreme, I define postmodern as incredulity toward metanarratives. . . . The narrative function is losing . . . its great hero, its great dan-

gers, its great voyages, its great goal. . . . Thus the society of the future falls less within the province of a Newtonian anthropology . . . than a pragmatics of language particles. There are many different language games—a heterogeneity of elements. They only give rise to institutions in patches—local determinism. . . . Postmodern language is not simply a tool of the authorities; it refines our sensitivity to differences and reinforces our ability to tolerate the incommensurable. (xxiv)

Postmodern discourse purports to "tolerate the incommensurable" by negating the notion of unity. In rejecting the possibility of shared methods of acquiring knowledge, common moral standards, and agreed-upon rules of communication, postmodernism produces the notion of difference. Consequently, Enlightenment and postmodern discourses share a similar method of arriving at philosophical concepts. Both rely upon a semiotic process that establishes the meaning of one term by means of the negation and devaluation of an opposite term. I call this process single dialectical. The single dialectic creates binary hierarchies between semiotically related concepts: the notion of unity could not be created without the exclusion of difference and, conversely, the notion of heterogeneity could not be produced without the exclusion of unity. Furthermore, whatever their position with regard to the possibility of truth, modern and postmodern philosophies also share a distrust, if not contempt, for commonly accepted opinion. It seems that the goal of philosophical discourse is to differentiate itself from common sense. The desire to be undogmatic gives rise to an impetus to offer counterintuitive answers to age-old existential questions.

A problem arises for those cultural critics and philosophers who believe that some commonsense opinions can be both interesting and plausible. Sometimes philosophy must elaborate and defend, rather than only criticize and transform, commonsense opinion. Of course, common sense itself is a very slippery concept that always depends in part upon a community that shares, debates and negotiates cultural assumptions. By "common sense," I mean a concept akin to Jürgen Habermas's "lifeworld," or set of shared and often implicit assumptions that make possible human communication and, sometimes, agreement. In *The Theory of Communicative Action*, Habermas posits that "The world gains objectivity as one and the same world for a community of speaking and acting subjects. . . . The abstract concept of the world is a necessary condition if communicatively acting subjects are to reach understanding among themselves about what takes place in the world or is to be effected in it. . . . This lifeworld is bounded by the totality of interpretations presupposed by members as background knowledge."[4]

Like the "lifeworld," the notion of common sense has two components, the first, which is particular and transient, and the second, which could be regarded as universal. Because semantic and cultural assumptions tend to vary personally, historically, and contextually, they are undeniably particular. At the same time, there is a universal element to the human condition that is established not so much by the identification of the common characteristics that all human beings share, as by the exclusion of all the qualities that are not, and probably never will be, human—such as humans will not be able to fly (naturally), attain immortality, or embody perfection. Consequently, the particular and universal elements of the human condition are inextricably interrelated. The qualities we associate with human nature can most plausibly be articulated only negatively, through the exclusion of particular qualities which we do not possess.

Now I would like to explain how I plan to combine both the particular and the universal elements of a "commonsense" understanding of ethics and epistemology by means of a dialectical process whose genealogy I trace to the Enlightenment.[5] While current philosophical discourse tends to polarize on the issue of truth into relativist and universalist positions—the most significant of which are, arguably, presented by Lyotard and Habermas—commonsense opinion suggests that the truth lies somewhere in between. It is a commonly shared assumption that human knowledge is limited and fallible but can be validated; that its truth-value lies between objectivism and relativism. Analogously, it is a commonly shared assumption that morality is neither relative nor universal. Cultural and personal differences generate different conceptions of right and wrong; nonetheless, most of us still want to be able to declare that some acts are always wrong. Perceiving the need for systematically defending some commonly held intuitions, practices and beliefs, several important scholars have begun to elaborate what I would call a philosophy of common sense. Roy Bhaskar,[6] Christopher Norris[7] and Richard Bernstein,[8] for instance, attempt to overcome the prevalent opposition between relative and objective standards for ethics and knowledge. They formulate theories that, much like commonsense belief, reject both philosophical extremes. In *The New Constellation*, a book devoted to an analysis of contemporary philosophy and theory, Bernstein states:

> With respect to basic ethico-political norms of critique, much of twentieth-century thinking has fluctuated between two extremes. There are those . . . who tell us that we must frankly acknowledge that there is not—and cannot be—any rational grounding of the basic ethical-political norms. . . . At the other extreme are those who claim that the project of rationally grounding norms is not only a viable one but can be carried out. . . . We seem to be drawn into a grand Either/Or: either there is a rational grounding of the norms of critique or the conviction that there is such a rational grounding is itself a self-deceptive illusion. . . . So the question arises, can we avoid these extremes? Is there some third way of understanding critique that avoids—passes between—the Scylla of "groundless critique" and the Charybdis of rationally grounded critique that "rests" upon illusory foundations? There are many who think that the achievement of the "postmodern" moment is to open up the space for new styles and genres of critique that avoid the extremes and twin dangers of this grand Either/Or. . . . Is there a new way of understanding and practicing critique that escapes this grand Either/Or? . . . This is . . . a central question that is at the very heart of modern/postmodern debates. (7–8)

My book juxtaposes and examines the resonance between Enlightenment and postmodern speculations about the nature of knowledge and ethics to offer one possible answer to Bernstein's question. I argue that Enlightenment philosophy has something to add to the contemporary thinking that appears to subvert it. The first part of the book considers the problem of truth-certainty as discussed by Kant in the *Critique of Pure Reason*, reformulated by d'Alembert in the "Discours préliminaire" and critiqued by Lyotard in *The Postmodern Condition*. The second part examines the intersection between ethics and epistemology in Enlightenment and contemporary discourses, including Denis Diderot's *Supplément au Voyage de Bougainville*, René de Chateaubriand's *Atala*, Frantz Fanon's *The Wretched of the Earth*, and Edward Said's *Orientalism* and *The World, the Text, and the Critic*. Rather than reading Enlightenment philosophy as observing a single dialectical process that eliminates all sources of doubt or multiplicity of moral beliefs, *Double Dialectics* shows that different kinds of Enlightenment discourse chart a nuanced path that mediates between relativism and objectivism to offer creative avenues of thought for contemporary ethical and epistemological problems.

We have already observed that the single dialectic describes a hierarchy between two opposed terms. To reiterate, such a model outlines the semiotic process whereby one term acquires a positive meaning by negating the qualities associated with another, opposite, term. Relying upon

INTRODUCTION

this logic, universalists create unity by negating differences, while, conversely, relativists create heterogeneity by eliminating unity. The single dialectic is therefore a process that establishes binary hierarchies. By way of contrast, a doubled dialectic describes the semiotic process whereby two terms acquire meaning by excluding from their definition qualities that are associated with an opposite term. Philosophers who pursue a double dialectical process in ethics and epistemology take as a point of departure two equally valued concepts—in this case, universalism and relativism—that eventually undergo sublation, or the incorporation of desirable qualities and the gradual negation of undesirable qualities, to arrive at ethical visions and models of knowledge that transcend both extremes. That is to say, double dialectical writers incorporate and negate selective aspects of both universalism and relativism in an effort to overcome this philosophical impasse.[9]

In the first chapter of *Double Dialectics*, I consider both the possibilities and the limits of postmodern thought in answering some of the fundamental questions of human existence posed by Enlightenment writers. Taking Jean-François Lyotard's *The Postmodern Condition* and *The Differend* to be significant examples of postmodern philosophy, I examine their epistemological and ethical arguments. Lyotard's works offer a thorough critique of Enlightenment universalist rationalism as well as a sophisticated elaboration of postmodern principles. More importantly, these texts help readers realize the necessity of Enlightenment ethics and epistemology. In criticizing the limits of Enlightenment thought, I argue, postmodern philosophy confronts its own limitations.

Such impasses are rooted in the philosophical ambitions of Enlightenment thought to validate the authority of reason and the certainty of human knowledge. Perhaps no Enlightenment text is more ambitious in this sense than Kant's *Critique of Pure Reason*, whose "Transcendental deduction" I analyze in the second chapter of this book. By using a dialectical process that selectively incorporates and negates aspects of both subjectivism and objectivism, Kant attempts to redeem the possibility of subjective truth. His concept of "the categories" aims to reconcile the notions of objective, *a priori* knowledge and subjective, *a posteriori* sense perception. Nonetheless, Kant's epistemology fails to explain satisfactorily the phenomenon of shared experience as well as the apparent order of human perception. Kant's theory cannot demonstrate how subjective vision coincides with objective knowledge, I argue, because it remains trapped in the single dialectical logic that it attempts to undo. That is to say, Kant's

Critique negates rationalist objectivism only by elevating a form of subjectivism to the level of objective truth. Kant thus inverts the conventional connotations of rationalist objectivism and skepticist subjectivism established by his predecessors—most notably, Leibnitz and Hume—without explaining why humans should trust subjective sense impressions.

By way of contrast, d'Alembert's introduction to the *Encylopédie* offers a more plausible account of shared and orderly perception than does Kant's *Critique*. Although it is interpreted by contemporary scholars as offering a defense of objectivist rationalism, the "Discours préliminaire" employs a double dialectical process to negate both objectivity and radical doubt. D'Alembert simultaneously demonstrates why human knowledge cannot be objective—since our perspective is by definition anthropocentric—and why it can be validated nonetheless. D'Alembert's text thus brings us to the threshold of some of the most important theories of knowledge—offered by critics such as Bhaskar, Norris, and Bernstein—that combine philosophical sophistication with intuition and common sense.

The second part of this book shifts focus from epistemological to ethical questions. Believing that the problem of moral relativism is one of the most significant issues of our times, I read Enlightenment and modern texts in search of a way to reconcile cultural differences with moral limits. Contemporary criticism has made the rejection of ethnocentric (and hence false) universalism a matter of common sense. While respect for cultural diversity has brought us to a position akin to moral relativism, most of us nonetheless uphold some moral absolutes. To frame the *aporia* between equally plausible relativist and universalist positions, the second part of my book considers the following question: How can moral philosophy take into account cultural relativism while also incorporating some universalist principles? This is precisely the issue confronted by the diverse narratives of Diderot, Chateaubriand, Fanon, and Said. Each of their texts poses different ethical questions and arrives at unique answers. They all share, however, a double dialectical logic that overcomes both moral relativism and universalism.

Diderot's *Supplément* raises the question of what attitude should one foster toward radically different societies and moral practices. The narrative, which consists of a series of fictional conversations, anecdotes, and speeches by French explorers and Tahitians, ultimately leads to the conclusion that one should reject both universalist morality (which it depicts as hypocritical and ethnocentric) and cultural relativism (which it depicts as untenable). The only way to claim the universality of one's own values, Diderot suggests, is, paradoxically, by respecting cultural differences, or the relative. To arrive at a moral equilibrium, the *Supplément* observes a double dialectical process. On the one hand, the narrative rejects (or negates) complete cultural relativism by upholding the superiority of one's own cultural values over those of others. On the other hand, the text also rejects (or negates) ethnocentric universalism by endorsing respect for the mores of a host society.

While the *Supplément* considers what moral attitude toward cultural difference is most appropriate, Chateaubriand's *Atala* broaches the problem of cultural relativism from an ontological perspective. The novel asks: what kind of human being is best prepared to represent an ethical attitude toward cultural difference? In raising this issue, *Atala* challenges the emerging Romantic view, popularized by Jean-Jacques Rousseau, that Western and Native American cultures are ethical opposites. While beginning *Atala* with the familiar contrast between savage nature and European culture, by the end of the novel Chateaubriand transforms this polarity into a more complex model of hybrid cultural identity. The hybrid being, Chateaubriand illustrates, is formed by means of a double dialectical narrative process. The allegorical figures of Atala and Chactas incorporate and reject elements of two so-called opposite cultures—the Spanish and the American Indian—which they value equally. A mixed cultural formation, the novel implies, leads hybrid characters to epitomize an ethical attitude toward cultural difference. More specifically, Chactas's and Atala's simultaneously critical and empathetic perspectives toward Spanish and American Indian societies enables them to negotiate cultural differences without lapsing into moral relativism.

While suggesting how cultures can balance mutual criticism and respect in the abstract, Diderot's and Chateaubriand's texts do not confront directly the historical and political problem of intercultural hierarchy. Modern and contemporary philosophy is perhaps the first to make readers keenly aware of the fact that mutual respect cannot exist between hierarchically positioned, colonial and colonized, societies. To examine this problem, I turn to one of the most significant considerations of the relation between universal ethics and cultural differences, provided by Fanon's *The Wretched of the Earth*. In the chapter "Concerning Violence," Fanon reveals that colonialism depends upon a single dialectical process. Only by negating the humanity of the native—and hence by depicting the native as inhuman—can settlers claim to embody the universal standard of civilization. To undo the logic of colonialism and reassert their humanity, Fanon further suggests, the natives must observe an opposite dialectical process that negates the humanity of the settlers. The author, however, is not satisfied with this single dialectical solution. As much as he argues for the necessity of violence in a colonial context, he also imagines a postcolonial world ruled by peaceful relations. In the most utopic moment of his text, Fanon doubles, and then overcomes, the single dialectical logic of both colonialism and postcolonialism. His theory of cultural interaction attempts to offer a model for not only understanding social inequality and antagonism, but also for overcoming them.

Any study of the problem of cultural relativism cannot ignore the groundbreaking scholarship of Edward Said. In particular, *Orientalism* and *The World, the Text, and the Critic* attune readers to the epistemological dimensions of ethics. These texts raise the important question of how nations can represent each other in a truthful and respectful manner. In the last chapter of my book, I bring the problem of cultural relativism into a contemporary context by examining two representative critiques of Said's work, provided by Denis Porter and Aijaz Ahmad. I argue that both Porter and Ahmad misread *Orientalism* as a single dialectical text that describes the Orient as the negation of the Occident. In my reading of *Orientalism*, I identify the textual moments that point to a way beyond binary and hierarchical distinctions between Western and non-Western societies. I show that Said's more nuanced depictions of Orientalist discourse observe a double dialectical process. In a double dialectic, the West defines itself by distinguishing itself from its cultural Others and, reciprocally, non-Western cultures also define themselves by negating Western qualities. While this process of reciprocal differentiation does not necessarily lead to intercultural equality, it provides a necessary step toward articulating cultural autonomy.

It is a cliché to observe that yesterday's counterintuitive philosophy becomes today's common sense. Common sense signifies the absence of critical judgment; the naive acceptance of presumably shared beliefs. The automatic rejection of former truths and current assumptions, however, constitutes as reflexive and unthoughtful a reaction as their dogmatic acceptance. The current rejection of much Enlightenment thought, which is based on a single dialectical interpretation of it as establishing rationalist objectivism by negating relativist considerations, has become the new critical orthodoxy. It is time that a new philosophical attitude toward our Enlightenment heritage, particularly regarding ethics and epistemology, emerge as common sense. My book outlines one such attitude by examining the correspondence between Enlightenment and contemporary speculations on the nature of knowledge and morality in terms of the dialectic. *Double Dialectics* illustrates that texts from vastly different ages, different genres, and responding to different intellectual debates and historical events, nonetheless share a common commitment to providing creative solutions to fundamental ethical and epistemological problems. Taking seriously the search for truthful representations of the world and livable moral visions, writers as vastly different as Kant, d'Alembert, Diderot, Chateaubriand, Fanon, and Said have not been satisfied with the poor alternative of choosing between relativist and universalist positions. Instead of adopting a single dialectical model that negates one extreme to support the other, their works observe a double dialectical process that rejects moral and epistemological absolutes while not abandoning the search for truth.

Reading Enlightenment and contemporary texts in terms of a dialectical logic that arrives at a path between relativism and universalism can contribute to the formation of what I regard as a timely philosophy of common sense. Being in part a product of the contemporary movement away from weighty philosophical systems, my elaboration of such a philosophy offers no specific answers. The double dialectical narrative logic that I identify in Enlightenment and contemporary texts cannot indicate what particular forms of knowledge qualify as negating both relativism and objectivism; what particular moral tenets count as both nonuniversalist and nonrelative. Instead of proposing a fully developed worldview, my reading of these texts in terms of the double dialectic outlines a general method of broaching philosophical questions that defend, rather than either automatically accepting or dismissing, some of the moral and epistemological assumptions that enable most of us to live from day to day.

Notes

1. I am using Paul Carus's translation of Kant's *Prolegomena to Any Future Metaphysics*.
2. I am using Norman Kemp's translation of Kant's *Critique of Pure Reason*.
3. I am using Geoff Bennington's and Brian Massumi's translation of Lyotard's *The Postmodern Condition: A Report on Knowledge*.
4. Habermas, *The Theory of Communicative Action*, vol. 1, 13.

5. Because my double dialectical reading of Enlightenment texts is only loosely related to the Frankfurt School's Marxist dialectical critique of modern society—only by virtue of employing a dialectical method, but not in the manner in which it employs it—I will not enter into direct dialogue with critical theory.

6. See Roy Bhaskar's *Reclaiming Reality: A Critical Introduction to Contemporary Philosophy*.

7. See Christopher Norris's *The Truth about Postmodernism* and *Reclaiming Truth: Contribution to a Critique of Cultural Relativism*.

8. See Richard Bernstein's *The New Constellation: The Ethical-Political Horizons of Modernity/Postmodernity*.

9. For a more detailed exposition of the distinction between the single and the double dialectics, see my book *Gender and Citizenship: The Dialectics of Subject-Citizenship in Nineteenth-Century French Literature and Culture*.

CHAPTER ONE

The Postmodern Need for a Philosophy of Common Sense: Lyotard's *The Postmodern Condition* and *The Differend*

By questioning the assumptions of traditional epistemology and ethics, postmodern philosophy casts doubt upon the certainties established by Enlightenment and modern thought.[1] We no longer believe, postmodernists tell us, that there is a stable, coherent, and rational self who observes the knowable and predictable (Newtonian) laws of nature. Once we reject the assumption that reason connects us to some universal truth, we also reject the belief that reason and science offer a stable foundation for knowledge and moral behavior. That is to say, if we are not motivated by the necessary and rational laws of nature, then our forms of knowledge are neither transcendental nor objectively true. Science loses authority as the paradigm of knowledge. The information we acquire, including scientific knowledge, is contingent, the product of partial and perhaps erroneous procedures. There is no guarantee that the information we obtain corresponds to anything true or real. In turn, if we do not attain absolute truth, then obeying the so-called laws of reason does not yield social and personal freedom and illumination. According to some postmodern critics, including Foucault and Lyotard, the discourse of truth represents only a highly effective means of exercising authority. There is no neutral form of knowledge: all knowledge is partial and self-serving. Knowledge is therefore socially beneficial only to those who know how to persuade by means of the most effective "language games." The claims made in the name of knowledge are validated only contextually, according to the rules and premises of a particular language game. Postmodern criticism thus tends to translate the discourse of truth into relations of power and claims about reality (things-in-themselves) into theories of representation (descriptions of reality).[2]

CHAPTER ONE

In this chapter I would like to consider both the possibilities and the limits of postmodernism in addressing some of the fundamental questions of human existence. Taking Jean-François Lyotard's main works, *The Postmodern Condition* and *The Differend*, to be significant examples of postmodern philosophy, I will briefly examine these texts with the following questions in mind: How does postmodernism represent the relation between truth and error? What are some of the blindspots of postmodern epistemology? What is the basis and nature of moral conduct according to postmodern philosophy? What are the limitations of postmodern ethics? I believe that Lyotard's works provide a good point of departure for broaching these questions not only because they offer a sophisticated elaboration of postmodern philosophy, but also because, in my estimation, they help readers realize the necessity of some of the Enlightenment tenets they reject. By this I do not mean to imply, as some critics do, that the shortcomings of postmodern theory make Enlightenment philosophy appear more appealing by comparison. Rather, I argue that postmodernism criticizes the limits of Enlightenment thought only to confront its own limitations. I will chart this philosophical route, which brings Enlightenment and postmodern philosophy to a full circle, by following Lyotard's shift from a single to a double dialectical model of epistemology and ethics.

In *The Postmodern Condition*, I argue, Lyotard pursues a single dialectical logic that negates objectivism to arrive at a relativist epistemology. In *The Differend*, the author attempts to follow the same relativist path by rejecting the assumptions that buttress universal morality and epistemological objectivity. By choosing to focus on the events of the Holocaust to substantiate his relativist theory, Lyotard illustrates that even in circumstances where universalism appears to be the only acceptable position—such as the observations that the Holocaust took place and that it was morally wrong—its assumptions and logic are open to questioning. In other words, by negating universalism even in one of its most compelling instantiations, *The Differend* seems to arrive at absolute relativism. Nonetheless, in my analysis of the chapter "The Differend," I will show that the text's conclusion is far from conclusive. In the chapter "The Referent, the Name," Lyotard in fact attempts to negate relativism and rebuild a shared epistemology and ethics upon nonuniversalist foundations. In so doing, he charts a double dialectical process similar to the one elaborated by the Enlightenment and modern texts we will examine. Enlightenment and postmodern discourses, rather than being only opposites, sometimes resonate in the effort to provide plausible answers to the most challenging human questions.

A Single Dialectical Epistemology: Lyotard's *The Postmodern Condition*

In *The Postmodern Condition: A Report on Knowledge*, Lyotard announces the beginning of a new era, characterized by the questioning of every discourse that aims to discover and communicate truth, including theology, science, social science, ethics and law. He defines the modern period as deploying "any science that legitimates itself with reference to a metadiscourse" (xxiii). By way of contrast, he describes the postmodern attitude as "an incredulity toward metanarratives" (xxiv). Postmodern culture undermines the certainties that enabled modern societies to function by "making an explicit appeal to some kind of grand narrative, such as the dialectics of Spirit, the hermeneutics of meaning, the emancipation of the rational or working subject, or the creation of wealth" (xxiii). According to the author, the fields of science, social science, and humanities, which began to be differentiated during the Enlightenment, are similarly governed by rhetorical operations that aim at reaching mutual understanding and consensus. In all cases, "truth-value is deemed acceptable if it is cast in terms of a possible unanimity between rational minds: this is the Enlightenment narrative, in which the hero of knowledge works toward a good ethico-political end—universal peace" (xxiv). Enlightenment metanarratives thus depend upon, and in fact generate, a subject of knowledge that is unified, coherent, rational and supposedly works toward a common goal with all other similarly constructed subjects.[3]

To arrive at such unity, Lyotard suggests, the self must eliminate (or negate) all logical inconsistencies, partial affiliations, disruptive psychological impulses, and social differences from its being and social context. In other words, the modern subject develops as a result of a single dialectical process that negates the fragmentation, incoherence, difference, and partiality that would disturb social unity and consensus. Consensus, Lyotard concludes, "does violence to the heterogeneity of language games. And invention is always born of dissension. Postmodern knowledge is not simply a tool of the authorities; it refines our sensitivity to differences and reinforces our ability to tolerate the incommensurable" (xxv). Lyotard clearly sets up a binary opposition between modern and postmodern discourse. Postmodern discourse represents everything that the Enlightenment attempted to eliminate from its system of thought; difference, heterogeneity, and disagreement. Since postmodern philosophy is generated by the negation of Enlightenment universalism, it stands to reason that postmodernism emerges from a homologous, but inverse, single dialectical process to the one that created Enlightenment concepts. That is to say, the heterogeneity and multiplicity of postmodern discourse is created by the elimination of the unity and consensus attributed to modern discourse. My question is: being a product of the same dialectical process, how is postmodern discourse an improvement over Enlightenment thought?

I raise this question because Lyotard clearly believes that postmodernism represents such an improvement. Just as numerous Enlightenment and modern philosophers, ranging from Condorcet to Marx, believed in the inevitable progress of the human being and society, so Lyotard believes in the inevitable dissemination of postmodern forms of knowledge. "The nature of knowledge cannot survive unchanged within this context of general transformation. It can fit into the new channels, and become operational, only if learning is translated into quantities of information" (4). Despite the heterogeneity of postmodern discourses, Lyotard suggests, all regimes of knowledge can be described in terms of a unitary theory of power: "Knowledge in the form of an informational commodity indispensable to productive power is already, and will continue to be, a major—perhaps *the* major—stake in the worldwide competition for power. . . . A new field is opened for industrial and commercial strategies on the one hand, and political and military strategies on the other" (5). While political interests, contexts, and linguistic rules may differ, the objective of all discourses remains the same: the manifestation of power. "For it appears in its most complete form, that of reversion, revealing that knowledge and power are simply two sides of the same question: who decides what knowledge is, and who knows what needs to be decided? In the computer age, the question of knowledge is now more than ever a question of government" (8–9). If all knowledge can be reduced to one overarching goal or effect, we are led to ask, then how does Lyotard's epistemology differ from the unitary epistemology he ascribes to modern thought? Lyotard addresses such a question by suggesting that the universalist discourse of the Enlightenment established itself upon the foundation of truth. By translating truth into power relations, postmodern philosophy dispels objective criteria of legitimation.

While not having the same foundations as modern discourse, postmodernism nonetheless produces similar effects. Both modern and postmodern discourses gain authority by distinguishing different communities and areas of competence from those who fall outside of their boundaries. By creating and then negating the difference of others, Lyotard maintains, privileged communities establish control over less privileged ones. So far, Lyotard is not saying anything different from Fanon or Said. He observes that some communities use knowledge to deny the humanity of others and thus establish social and moral authority. At the same time, he generalizes Fanon's and Said's observations. According to Lyotard, all discourses are equally complicit—even if differently effective—in the quest for power. From this assumption it follows, for instance, that colonialist and anticolonialist discourses are equally right or wrong. Discourses that claim to espouse truth and moral correctness, Lyotard further suggests, only aim to produce social hierarchies: "What is a 'good' prescriptive or evaluative utterance, a 'good' performance in denotative or technical matters? They are all judged to be 'good' because they conform to the relevant critieria (of justice, beauty, truth, and efficiency respectively) accepted in the social circle of the 'knower's' interlocutors. . . . The consensus that permits such knowledge to be circumscribed and makes it possible to distinguish one who knows from one who doesn't (the foreigner, the child) is what constitutes the culture of a people" (19).

Postmodern philosophy exercises its own demystifying form of power to undo the influence of universalism. To distinguish postmodernism from its philosophical precursors, Lyotard insists that he is only depicting a cultural process that is already under way rather than prescribing what should occur. "In contemporary society and culture—postindustrial society, postmodern culture—the question of the legitimation of knowledge is formulated in different terms. The grand narrative has lost its credibility, regardless of what mode of unification it uses, regardless of whether it is a speculative narrative or a narrative of emancipation" (37). Since the Second World War, Lyotard observes, the dissemination of technology has encouraged Western societies to focus on pragmatic aspects of life. Modern cultures have given up the search for a universal truth that is not related to immediate results. Consequently, in the wake of modernization, a new pragmatics of knowledge has emerged. This way of life is made possible by a multiplicity of language games that are "heteromorphous, subject to heterogeneous sets of pragmatic rules" (65). Because postmodern societies have abandoned the search for universal truth, Lyotard reasons, ". . . it seems neither possible, nor even prudent, to follow Habermas in orienting our treatment of the problem of legitimation in the direction of a search for universal consensus" (65). My question is: does Lyotard's description of postmodernism circularly arrive at universalism by means of an opposite route?

Given that he has translated both epistemology and ethics into a unitary theory of power, Lyotard has undermined the supposed heterogeneity of postmodern narratives. While seeming to negate the concepts of sameness, unity, and consensus to proclaim the value of difference, postmodern philosophy arrives at something resembling a common cause, which levels the differences among postmodern discourses. The problem with Lyotard's version of postmodernism stems from its single dialectical negation of universalism. By setting postmodernism in direct opposition to universalism, Lyotard replaces the modern discourse of value (truth, right) with a postmodern discourse of power that is similarly unitary. In pursuing this single dialectical logic, Lyotard's rendition of postmodern philosophy is no more equipped to distinguish among (the ideological effects of) postmodern discourses than he is attuned to the nuances of Enlightenment and modern thought (which he dismisses as universalist). The need to distinguish among discourses, however, becomes all the more obvious when claims about truth intersect with assumptions about morality. This is precisely the problem with which Lyotard grapples in his later book, *The Differend: Phrases in Dispute*.[4]

The Need for Double Dialectics: Lyotard's *The Differend*

The Differend examines the foundation of ethics by intertwining in a surprising dialogue radically different kinds of relativist and universalist discourses. The text places side by side citations from Plato's *Gorgias* with articles from Nazi revisionist historians and journal excerpts from Holocaust victims. To increase the confusion, the citations are removed from their textual and historical contexts. What is the reader to make of this pastiche of historical information intermingled with philosophical speculations about the nature of morality and knowledge? This is precisely the question raised by *The Differend*. To induce readers to think about their ethical and epistemological assumptions, Lyotard begins by defamiliarizing moral discourse. His presentation of ethical problems is not only unconventional, but also downright shocking. While some critics celebrate *The Differend* as a highlight of postmodern philosophy, others express a sense of outrage at its unabashed ethical relativism. Christopher Norris is one of the most outspoken critics of postmodern philosophy. In his essay "Kant Disfigured," Norris cautions:

> [M]oral relativism if taken seriously can offer no defence against obnoxious creeds just so long as there is (or once was) a "language-game," "discourse" or cultural "form of life" wherein they enjoyed some measure of communal assent. . . . Only thus can one explain Lyotard's attitude in the face of right-wing "revisionist" arguments like that of Robert Faurisson, namely, that since no witnesses survive who can vouch directly for what happened inside the gas-chambers at Auschwitz, therefore the historical record is mute on this point and we should treat all talk of the Holocaust as—so far as we can possibly know—a conspiracy devised to denigrate the Nazis and promote the Zionist cause. The most obvious response to such sophistries would be to point out their manifestly absurd major premise, their willful disregard for other (massively documented) sources of knowledge, and the presence of a blatant motivating interest, or crudely propagandist intent, which explains both their flouting of their factual-historical rules of evidence and their utterly unprincipled ethical stance. (249)

Whether one is impressed with or outraged by Lyotard's approach to ethics, the question remains: Why does the author choose to buttress postmodern ethics on one of the most sensitive examples of the need for universalist thought? An obvious answer would be that the true test of moral relativism is its response to incidents that seem unquestionably evil. This explanation, however, does not fully explain *The Differend*'s ability to provoke readers. For not only does the text level the distinction between right and wrong, it also inverts this relation by expressing moral disapproval at the suppression of what are conventionally regarded as immoral points of view. Norris continues:

> For Lyotard, however, such [moral] arguments are beside the point, assuming as they do that Faurisson is playing by the same evidential or ethical rules, or that opponents have the right to arraign this "discourse" from a standpoint of assuredly superior probity and truth. By so doing, Lyotard maintains, they commit an injustice, a suppression of the "differend," which deprives their case of any genuine claim to rectify Faurisson's similar breach of ethico-discursive responsibility. This seems to me a very clear (and shocking) example of what can go wrong when moral relativism is joined to an extreme version of the

> incommensurability thesis derived from post-structuralist and other theoretical sources. For the result of such thinking is to level the difference between truth and falsehood, good and bad faith, respect for other people's honestly-argued convictions and an attitude of all-purpose skeptical doubt which admits any viewpoint—however ill-founded, prejudicial or malign—as entitled to its own internal criteria. (249–50)

I cite Norris's position at length because I am highly sympathetic to it. Having had a similar reaction to *The Differend*, I searched, however, for a different way to defend the commonsense opinion that some acts, including the murder of millions of people, are evil. To do so, I will turn Lyotard's text against itself. My reading of *The Differend* will reveal that, unlike the earlier *Postmodern Condition*, this text does not stop at the rejection of universalist values to support moral relativism. Rather, in the chapter by the same name, *The Differend* turns full circle and calls for the creation of new moral boundaries. Such moral limits, Lyotard cautions, cannot be established upon universalist foundations, which, as noted, he believes are only a product of power relations. To arrive at a nonuniversalist postmodern ethic, Lyotard pursues a double dialectical process that negates both universalism and relativism. I will argue, however, that Lyotard never presents this new moral order—nor does the narrative logic of his text help readers envision it—because he does not perform a full sublation of both relativism and universalism. That is to say, *The Differend* incorporates and negates aspects of relativism while only negating aspects of universalism.

To understand the path that Lyotard attempts to chart between relativism and universalism, let us first see what the author means by "the differend." Lyotard offers three definitions of the term, all of which pertain to a pragmatic, legal context. Ethics and law, the author suggests, are inextricably intertwined. Ethics serves as the foundation of law, while law provides the concrete framework for the negotiation and enforcement of ethical values. The differend occurs when ethical values cannot be negotiated because of the absence of agreed-upon laws. In the first instance, "a differend would be a case of conflict between (at least) two parties, that cannot be equitably resolved for lack of rule of judgment applicable to both arguments. One side's legitimacy does not imply the other's lack of legitimacy" (xi). A common example of such a situation would be the political debates of the United Nations. In the absence of any higher judge or agreed-upon law, there is no way to resolve the moral and political conflicts that result from cultural and personal differences without excluding, and thus wronging, some nations.

The second example of an insoluble moral conflict is "the case where the plaintiff is divested of the means to argue and becomes for that reason a victim" (9). To be able to adjudicate a moral conflict, Lyotard suggests, we need not only shared laws, but also the fair presentation of the conflict itself. When one side cannot speak for itself and affect the judgment of the arbiter or judge as much as the other side, the moral conflict becomes undecidable. This description of the differend leads us to the third meaning of the term. Sometimes a legal conflict cannot be decided equitably because the judge or jury is biased. While unbiased judgment is certainly assumed in the legal systems of democratic nations, Lyotard suggests, such fairness is an unattainable regulative ideal. Given that ethical evaluation in a legal context is always biased, Lyotard asks, what becomes of moral judgment?

To answer this question, the author turns to the epistemological basis of moral judgment. Legal systems may be imperfect, but human beings have other ways of distinguishing right from wrong. Much as Hume systematically undermined confidence in causal reasoning, so Lyotard turns to epistemology to unravel commonsense assumptions about what constitutes adequate proof. Furthermore, just as Hume demonstrated that causal reasoning may lead us to plausible, but far from certain conclusions, so Lyotard wants to demonstrate that legal evidence only shows that an event probably occurred. There is no way to prove a crime occurred and to identify with certainty the perpetrator. If ethics has no certain epistemological foundation that supports alleged facts, Lyotard further suggests, then normative judgments are arbitrary.

Lyotard's testing ground for the intersection between epistemology and ethics is the following question: How can we prove that a horrific historical event—such as the Holocaust—took place? Furthermore, Lyotard pursues, given the manner in which we are able to prove that this event happened, how can we judge it as right or wrong? Assuming that epistemology and ethics are two facets of the same universalist coin, Lyotard attempts to invalidate proofs that the Holocaust took place—by showing the shaky ground on which such proofs rest—to unsettle our confidence in moral judgments.

He begins by juxtaposing two kinds of narratives that declare truth-certainty: the traditional historical account, which argues that the Holocaust took place and that it was evil, versus the Nazi revisionist account, which states that there is no evidence of the Holocaust. Both traditional and Nazi historians, Lyotard suggests, pursue a single dialectical process to establish the certainty of their conclusions. As we recall, a single dialectical narrative depends upon the creation of binary hierarchies. Following this logic, traditional historians rely upon different kinds of evidence to negate all doubts and support the position that the Holocaust certainly happened. Homologously, Nazi historians reject all evidence to invalidate proofs of the Holocaust.

By way of contrast, Lyotard's *Differend* observes a double dialectical logic that gives both universalism and relativism equal value. Both objectivists and relativists, Lyotard suggests, cannot fully substantiate their arguments. This is perhaps the most disturbing element of Lyotard's text: while many individuals with different political agendas have denied the existence of the Holocaust, few have suggested that traditional and Nazi accounts of this event are equally (in)valid. To chart this double dialectical path between complete certainty and doubt, Lyotard considers the occurrence of the Holocaust from an epistemological and ontological perspective.

Epistemology: Negating Truth-Certainty

Traditional historical accounts of the Holocaust generally rely upon three types of narrative evidence: a) the testimony of Holocaust survivors and victims; b) the testimony of eyewitnesses; and c) interpretations of victims' trauma and resulting silence. As noted, Lyotard juxtaposes such accounts with the denials of Nazi revisionist historians to invalidate both arguments.

Personal Experience

Lyotard begins by analyzing evidence based upon personal experience, including diaries such as the one written by Anne Frank. Personal accounts are assumed to be at least partially generalizable. That is to say, traditional historians argue that the experience of one individual can say something about the experience of others. By way of contrast, Nazi historians reject this assumption. They present the following argument: "You are informed that human beings endowed with language were placed in a situation such that none of them is now able to tell about it. When they do speak about it, their testimony bears only upon a minute part of this situation" (3). While traditional historians maintain that the testimony of Holocaust survivors provides reliable evidence of what millions of other victims experienced, Nazi revisionist historians assert that it is unique to the experience of that single victim. Lyotard selectively rejects and incorporates elements of both arguments. *The Differend* suggests that historians must be particularly careful about making generalizations based upon personal experience without going so far as to conclude that personal narratives can never be generalized. Lyotard's juxtaposition of two positions that claim truth-certainty raises the question: to what degree is personal experience and narration reliable evidence for a mass phenomenon? Leaving this question open for the reader to decide, Lyotard moves on to consider the credibility of the victim.

A second issue that presents itself in the evaluation of personal evidence is the problem of truth-value. Is the personal account a true, undistorted, representation of the facts? While traditional historians argue that personal accounts of Holocaust victims are reliable, Nazi historians argue that any exaggeration or distortion made in that document renders a personal account completely untrue. Once again, to offer my own example, Anne Frank's diary provides a good example for this debate. Traditional historians have found that Anne distorted many minor facts. Anne herself admitted that she exaggerated the negative depiction of her mother and of the members of the family who shared her hiding place. Traditional historians nonetheless argue that such exaggerations have no bearing on Anne's experience as a Nazi victim. The fact that she might have exaggerated descriptions of her mother has nothing to do with the fact that she had to hide to survive; that she experienced food shortages; that she eventually died in a concentration camp. All these events, historians argue, remain undeniably true. Nazi historians use the same information to reach the opposite conclusion. In their estimation, any distortion of facts damages irreparably the credibility of the witness. Consequently, they suggest, nothing Anne wrote in her diary can be trusted. "How can you know that the situation itself existed? That it is not the fruit of your informant's imagination?" they disingenuously ask (3). Lyotard's narrative once again distances itself, or negates, both objectivist and relativist positions. Personal evidence, *The Differend* suggests, is neither completely reliable nor unreliable. It is simply inconclusive. Readers therefore continually oscillate between belief and disbelief. Having sublated these two opposing positions, the text moves on to consider a second type of evidence.

CHAPTER ONE

Witnesses, Empirical Evidence, and Logic

Most victims of the Holocaust did not live to write or tell about it. Much of the evidence of mass murders that occurred was gathered from eyewitnesses, from the individuals who saw the horror or were asked to work in the concentration camps. The Nazi historians, however, attempt to invalidate eyewitness accounts by constructing the following syllogism:

> To have "really seen with his own eyes" a gas chamber would be the condition which gives one the authority to say that it exists and to persuade the unbeliever. Yet it is still necessary to prove that the gas chamber was used to kill at the time it was seen. The only acceptable proof that it was used to kill is that one died from it. But if one is dead, one cannot testify that it is on account of the gas chamber. . . . [In] order for a place to be identified as a gas chamber, the only eyewitness I will accept would be a victim of this gas chamber; now, according to my opponent, there is no victim that is not dead; otherwise, this gas chamber would not be what he or she claims it to be. There is, therefore, no gas chamber. (3–4)

Nazi historians take as their major premise the assumption that the only way to prove that the gas chambers killed is to have experienced death under those circumstances. Their minor premise is that all individuals who experienced the gas chambers are dead. A second minor premise is that if a victim is dead, he or she cannot speak about it. This chain of reasoning leads them to the conclusion that the fact that the gas chambers were used to kill people cannot be substantiated. Obviously, there are many shaky premises in this chain of reasoning. For instance, the assumption that only those who died in a gas chamber can attest to its existence and use is clearly false. Nonetheless, sophistical logic can lead to the relativist conclusion that, "since the only witnesses are the victims, and since there are no victims but dead ones, no place can be identified as a gas chamber" (5). *The Differend* does not side with the Nazi revisionist historians to suggest that the Holocaust is conclusively unprovable. Nor does it side with traditional historians who trust eyewitness accounts. Rather, *The Differend* provides a metacritique of the conceptual tools that enable both sides to make their arguments. Logic, Lyotard shows, can be a double-edged knife that can lead to opposing conclusions. Rather than being an instrument of truth, as objectivists assume, logic is a rhetorical tool. Suspending readers once again between certainty and doubt, Lyotard moves on to consider the third type of evidence.

The Undecidability of Silence

Individuals who experienced the Holocaust expressed themselves in different ways. A few wrote about it. Most survivors, however, internalized their pain and remained silent. For historians of the Holocaust, what is not said about this event is as important as what is said about it. The fact that many Holocaust survivors find their memories too painful for words, indicates to many the extent of their suffering. According to Nazi historians, however, not speaking about the Holocaust implies that no suffering occurred: "The survivors remain silent, and it can be understood 1) that the situation in question is not the addressee's business; or 2) that it never took place; or 3) that there is nothing to say about it; or 4) that it is not the survivor's business to be talking about it. Or several of these negations together" (14). Rejecting both historical interpretations, Lyotard uses Plato's *Gorgias* to argue that silence represents a double bind: "The silence of the survivors does not necessarily testify in favor of the nonexistence of gas chambers, as Faurisson [the Nazi historian] believes or pretends to believe. It can just as well testify against the addressee's authority . . . , against the authority of the witness . . . , finally against language's ability to signify gas chambers (as an inexpressible absurdity)" (14). Faced with silence, the public cannot decide between several plausible but mutually exclusive meanings.

Ontology: Negating Physical Evidence

Having considered the difficulty of proving that an event occurred based upon verbal and narrative evidence, Lyotard moves on to evaluate the most compelling and gruesome proof of the Holocaust: the gas chambers themselves, the trains used to transport millions of people to their deaths, the bits of clothing and hair found in concentration camps, the photographs of emaciated victims. In the second chapter of *The Differend*, entitled "The Referent, the Name," Lyotard examines the nature of physical evidence. Although I will not analyze the rest of Lyotard's text here, I would like to signal some of its main arguments to indicate how the author continues his

CHAPTER ONE

dialectical path between relativism and universalism. Lyotard first maintains that proofs of reality generally depend upon circular arguments. Tautological arguments tend to run as follows: "I say the gas chambers exist because they were there." Such arguments, Lyotard implies, do not demonstrate anything. From tautologies, "Existence is not concluded. The ontological argument is false. Nothing can be said about reality that does not presuppose it" (32).

A second manner in which people substantiate claims about reality is by offering numerous details. The ability to produce details generally convinces individuals that an event occurred. Yet, Lyotard succinctly objects, "Naming is not showing" (33). Details may signal an active imagination rather than proving that an event occurred. Lyotard's third ontological argument challenges the belief in the continuity of the subject. Alluding to Descartes's method of radical doubt, Lyotard suggests that there may be no continuity between subjects who were alive in the gas chambers and those who died a few moments later. "The possibility of reality, including the reality of the subject, is fixed in networks of names 'before' reality shows itself and signifies itself in experience" (35). Relatedly, Lyotard proceeds to argue, claims about reality are always vague, if not indecipherable, because language itself is undecidable. Applying Saussurean linguistics to ethical problems, Lyotard indicates that in a diacritical system of language, "Reality is not expressed therefore by a phrase like: *x is such*, but by one like: *x is such and not such*. To the assertion of reality, there corresponds a description inconsistent with regard to negation. This inconsistency characterizes the modality of the possible" (45). If we accept Saussure's argument that human beings communicate by moving from one linguistic approximation (or signified) to another, Lyotard suggests, we are led to the conclusion that we do not have access to the referent (or prelinguistic reality) in itself.

What is left of proofs of the Holocaust? If one lends credence to Lyotard's reading, there are no traces of concentration camps; there is no verifiable history:

> Is it up to the historian to take into account not only the damages, but also the wrong? Not only the reality, but also the meta-reality that is the destruction of reality? Not only the testimony, but also what is left of the testimony when it is destroyed (by dilemma), namely, the feeling? Not only the litigation, but also the differend? . . . Auschwitz is the most real of realities. . . . Its name marks the confines wherein historical knowledge sees its competence im-

pugned. It does not follow from that that one falls into non-sense. The alternative is not: either the signification that learning (*science*) establishes, or absurdity, be it of the mystical kind. (57–58)

To talk about the Holocaust, Lyotard suggests, we must invent new rules of validation that take into account the fact that nothing can be either proved or disproved with absolute certainty. This is certainly a commonsense conclusion—pursued, for instance, by American courts in the clause that a person is declared guilty when the jury is certain beyond reasonable doubt that the accused perpetrated the crime. Nonetheless, Lyotard's interpretation of a double dialectical process, as well as the epistemological and ethical claims he makes, lead to shocking conclusions. As the author himself suggests, the process of negating both relativism and universalism risks falling "into non-sense." Indeed, the conclusion that the Holocaust may not have occurred, that there is no way for historians to prove that it did, is altogether nonsensical. For just as we go to bed each evening expecting to wake up in the morning at the light of the sun—even though, as Hume indicated, we cannot be absolutely sure that the sun will rise—so our societies must function as if some of their most deeply-held moral and epistemological convictions were true.

I have argued that *The Differend* attempts to chart a path between relativism and universalism to create a distinctly postmodern epistemology and ethics. To do so, Lyotard pursues an incomplete double dialectical process that selectively negates and incorporates elements of relativism—and, indeed, arrives at similar conclusions to those of Nazi revisionist historians—without also incorporating elements of universalism. In assessing the reliability of evidence, *The Differend* never incorporates some universalist tenets—such as the criteria needed to distinguish between essential and nonessential facts. According to the logic of Lyotard's reading, Anne Frank's exaggerations about the boy she fell in love with are as important as if she had lied about hiding from the Nazis. The same can be said about Lyotard's juxtaposition of logical arguments made by traditional historians and Nazi revisionist historians. Having only negated universalism without also incorporating some objectivist standards—such as the distinction between true and false (or plausible and implausible) premises—Lyotard dismantles logic to arrive at a syllogism which resembles that of the Nazi historians. Postmodern critics might respond that the distinctions between significant and insignificant evidence or between true and false assumptions are a product of objectivist language games.

While this may be true, I would respond in turn that without such assumptions we cannot function as human societies and risk, as Lyotard himself cautions, "falling into non-sense."

Rather than observing a dialectical process to return to a new, "postmodern" relativism, contemporary critics are beginning to use a double dialectical logic to reevaluate commonsensical positions and overcome the impasse between relativism and universalism. This philosophical common sense carries with it its own risks. As we have seen, by negating universalism, Lyotard's *Differend* reverted to conventional relativism. Similarly, if contemporary critics negate relativism and incorporate universalist positions too readily, their philosophies risk lapsing into dogma. *Double Dialectics* will not provide any formulaic solution to this dilemma. My reading of Enlightenment and contemporary theories in terms of the logic of the dialectic will offer a method for understanding local answers to the difficult quest for a philosophical equilibrium between universalism and relativism.

Notes

1. For a succinct explanation of how postmodern theory undermines the tenets of modern philosophy, see Linda Nicholson and Nancy Fraser's "Social Criticism without Philosophy" and Jane Flax's "Postmodernism and Gender Relations" in *Feminism/Postmodernism*.

2. For further introductions to postmodern thought, see Raman Selden's *A Reader's Guide to Contemporary Literary Theory*, Madan Sarup's *An Introductory Guide to Post-Structuralism and Postmodernism* and James Good and Irving Velody's (editors) *The Politics of Postmodernity*.

3. In this citation, Lyotard is alluding (and objecting) to Jürgen Habermas's theory of communicative action.

4. I am using Georges Van Den Abbeele's translation of Lyotard's *The Differend: Phrases in Dispute*.

CHAPTER TWO

Dialectical Deduction: A Reading of Kant's *Critique of Pure Reason*

Written in the midst of the Enlightenment debate between objectivist rationalism and empiricist skepticism, Immanuel Kant's *Critique of Pure Reason* (1781)[1] attempts to offer a solution to the problem of how humans can verify the truth-certainty of their empirical and analytical knowledge. Kant aims to avoid the difficulties inherent in both objectivism and subjectivism, the dominant philosophical currents of his time. On the one hand, Kant rejects René Descartes's and G. W. Leibnitz's proposition that humans can attain true knowledge of the universe by utilizing their rational faculties. He finds such rationalism not only presumptuous, but also unsubstantiated. On the other hand, Kant also rejects George Berkeley's idealism and David Hume's empiricist skepticism, both of which (differently) undermine the possibility of truth. While Berkeley suggests that reality consists of our subjective ideas of objects rather than of things-in-themselves, Hume questions the foundation of human knowledge by casting doubt upon causal reasoning. Because Kant attempts to overcome the impasse between objectivism and subjectivism, it is not surprising that contemporary critics who are interested in epistemological problems, including Michel Foucault, Jean-François Lyotard, and Jürgen Habermas, have turned to his works for inspiration and critique. Kant addresses the following questions: What is the nature of human knowledge? How can humans know that what we perceive or think is true? If we cannot be certain of our knowledge, does it follow that we must consider all knowledge as equal in validity or even reject the possibility of truth?

Kant's epistemology remains both useful and challenging to contemporary scholarship that grapples with the issue of truth-certainty because, I will argue,[2] he searches for a dialectical solution to the impasse between skepticist relativism and rationalist objectivism. Whereas Kantian scholars tend to interpret Kant's epistemology as either idealist-subjectivist or realist-objectivist, I will demonstrate that Kant's epistemology conforms to neither extreme. For instance, arguing against Henry Allison's *Kant's Transcendental Idealism*,[3] which posits that Kant's idealism is tautological and thus intrinsically nonidealist, James Van Cleeve maintains that "to the contrary . . . he is an honest-to-goodness idealist regarding the entire world in space and time."[4] Van Cleeve wishes to prove that in Kant's epistemology, "the object conforms to our knowledge rather than vice versa. Such is Kant's Copernican Revolution in philosophy" (5). By way of contrast, Arthur W. Collins[5] attempts to prove that Kant's transcendental idealism has nothing to do with the idealist tradition, and everything to do with a realist-objectivist conception of the world, whereby our perception of objects is at least partially based on their true nature: "Kant does not merely fail to take a solipsistic outlook; he argues that such a starting point cannot possibly exist. We are conscious at all, Kant holds, only because we are conscious of things outside our minds" (7). The problem which Collins must resolve is not an easy one: namely, what is the relation between our perceptions and true reality in Kant's philosophy?

If the critics who argue that Kant is an idealist encounter problems with his conception of a noumenal or true reality and, conversely, the critics who argue that Kant is an objectivist-realist encounter problems with the tenuous connection he establishes between human perception and true reality, it is because interpreting Kant's philosophy as either idealist or realist-objectivist does not capture the intrinsic dialectical tension of its theory of knowledge. Perhaps because of this tension, which I will explore in this chapter, a great number of Kantian scholars abandon both interpretive extremes and focus instead upon the puzzling tensions of Kant's transcendental idealism.[6] Most notably, H. W. Cassirer draws attention to the irreconcilable contradictions of Kant's dualist epistemology.[7] He observes,

> But Kant realizes that the whole realm of the given is permeated by space and time, so that it is made impossible to find anywhere, within the field of sensible phenomena, anything which could be regarded as solidly real and independent of mind in the required sense. This is one of the reasons why he postulates a supersensible realm, a realm of things-in-themselves, while affirming that these things-in-themselves are to be held to be ultimately re-

sponsible for the element of reality in the sense given. This device of Kant's seems to me to introduce more difficulties than it solves, especially since he himself admits that supersensible things are quite unknowable, and that the reality which would pertain to them must be considered to be fundamentally different from that which pertains to the objects of sense-experience. (37)

To explain the nature of these tensions and polarities in Kantian epistemology, I will trace Kant's attempts to overcome the single dialectical opposition between objectivism and subjectivism, each being defined as not the other. The philosopher rejects the assumption that truth requires the negation of all subjective knowledge and, conversely, that subjectivism entails the negation of objective truth. By using a dialectical process that selectively incorporates and negates aspects of both subjectivism and objectivism, I argue, Kant creates an epistemology that attempts to redeem the possibility of subjective truth. He proposes to reconcile objective, *a priori* knowledge and subjective, *a posteriori* sense perception by "explain[ing] the possibility of knowing *a priori*, by means of categories, whatever objects may present themselves to our senses, not indeed in respect of the form of their intuition, but in respect of the laws of their combination, and so, as it were, of prescribing laws to nature, and even making nature possible" (*Critique*, 170).

Kant considers the crucial question of whether human faculties produce a shared reality or, on the contrary, whether the regularity of the laws of nature makes possible shared and orderly perceptions. The author responds to this question in a surprising and new way. He suggests that knowledge is provided by "the categories" of our minds that translate the external reality into comprehensible and shared human perception. Rejecting both Leibnitz's rationalist objectivism and Hume's skepticist subjectivism, Kant maintains that "A middle course may be proposed between the two above mentioned, namely, that the categories are neither self-thought first principles *a priori* of our knowledge nor derived from experience, but subjective dispositions of thought, implanted in us from the first moment of our existence, and so ordered by our Creator that their employment is in complete harmony with the laws of nature with which experience proceeds—a kind of preformation-system of pure reason" (*Critique*, 174–75).

By means of a dialectical sublation, Kant wants to demonstrate that subjective truth coincides with objective knowledge.[8] The path Kant charts between subjectivism and objectivism is notoriously complicated and counterintuitive. His hypothesis that the understanding is the lawgiver of nature implies that intuitions as we receive them are not ordered, or else that they are ordered in a way that does not bear a determinate relation to the regularity of our experience. If one accepts the commonsense assumption that nature operates according to laws that are independent of our minds and that these laws determine the regularity of our experience, however, it is difficult to accept Kant's theory of knowledge. A more widely-shared hypothesis is that the order of sensory perception is ultimately determined by whatever is the source of our intuitions, the most likely candidate being external reality or "things-in-themselves." The objection that a philosophical system is counterintuitive, however, is weak when applied to speculative thought.

The real argument I would like to develop is that Kant's epistemology does not provide elegant answers to the following two fundamental questions: 1) why does reality as we perceive it seem ordered if, as Kant argues, things-in-themselves produce chaotic sensory impressions and, 2) why do subjective impressions more or less coincide in different people perceiving the same object if knowledge has no basis in that external reality. I maintain that insofar as Kant fails to offer an elegant solution to the impasse between subjectivism and objectivism, it is because he remains trapped within the same single dialectical logic that he attempts to undo. By this I mean that Kant inverts the traditional hierarchy between objectivism and subjectivism without sublating their opposition. He negates rationalist objectivism only by elevating a form of subjectivism to the level of objective truth. He does not, in my estimation, fully succeed in refuting Hume's skepticism while at the same time offering a plausible explanation of regular perception and shared experience.

Epistemological Debates: Transcendental Idealism versus Empiricist Skepticism

Before turning to Kant's *Critique*, let me contextualize his argument by describing briefly the philosophical debates it addressed. I will focus in particular on the debate between the rationalist objectivist and subjectivist skeptical positions, most notably represented, respectively, by Leibnitz and Hume. As a rationalist objectivist, Leibnitz posits that true knowledge of the universe can be derived from our analytical rational faculties. Innate principles, according to Leibnitz, give us knowledge of the way the universe actually is, not only of how we subjectively perceive it. Although each thinking substance, which Leibnitz calls a "monad," does not interact with others, the monads are harmoniously interrelated by the preestablished rational order of the universe. Leibnitz thus defines objective knowledge in terms of a single dialectical process. For him, objective truth consists of the absence (or negation) of both subjective and intersubjective knowledge.

Although Kant was provoked by Leibnitz's rationalist objectivism, he was much more compelled by Hume's empiricist skepticism. Hume's epistemology pursues an inverse single dialectical process to undermine objective knowledge. In contradistinction to Leibnitz, Hume did not believe that the universe functions in accordance with a preestablished order. Nor did he believe that the way humans perceive the world corresponds to the way the universe is. Knowledge, he claimed, is derived primarily from experience. Because it is dependent upon perception, knowledge is deeply influenced by the perspective of the knower. Claims to objectivity are based upon causal reasoning, which is conditioned by habit rather than logic. When scientists, for instance, maintain that the laws of nature operate as they describe them, all they are saying is that nature behaves with a kind of constancy and coherence that seems to be independent of human perception. In denying [or negating] the possibility of objective knowledge, Hume's theory espouses a "moderate skepticism," which could be called subjectivist.

Kant was drawn to Hume's skepticism not only because it refuted the entrenched objectivist rationalism, but also because of its nondogmatic nature. Hume's *Enquiries Concerning Human Understanding and Concerning the Principles of Morals*[9] engages readers in a genuine quest for knowledge. Hume maintains that "The sweetest and most inoffensive path of life leads through the avenues of science and learning; and whoever can either remove any obstructions in this way, or open up any new prospect, ought so far to be esteemed a benefactor to mankind" (11). While pursuing radically different paths, Hume and Kant would share similar philosophical goals.

Hume's empiricism begins with the assumption that general or abstract ideas are extrapolated from empirical observations. "Or, to express myself in philosophical language," Hume elaborates,

> all our ideas or more feeble perceptions are copies of our impressions or more lively ones.... Even those ideas, which, at first view, seem the most wide of

> this origin, are found, upon a nearer scrutiny, to be derived from [a preceding feeling or sentiment]. The idea of God, as meaning an infinitely intelligent, wise, and good Being, arises from reflecting on the operations of our own mind, and augmenting, without limit, those qualities of goodness and wisdom. (Hume, *Enquiries*, 19)

According to Hume, all rational knowledge can be divided into two types: relations of ideas and matters of fact. Relations of ideas, such as logical deductions, do not depend upon the existence of external objects. By way of contrast, matters of fact are entirely contingent upon our observations of the external world. Rationalist philosophers, Hume maintains, mistakenly endow matters of fact with the same objective truth-value as they do relations of ideas. "Matters of fact," however,

> which are the second objects of human reason, are not ascertained in the same manner; nor is our evidence of their truth, however great, of a like nature with the foregoing. The contrary of every matter of fact is still possible; because it can never imply a contradiction, and is conceived by the mind with the same facility and distinctness, as if ever so conformable to reality. (*Enquiries*, 25–26)

Hume argues that we cannot claim that *a posteriori* matters of fact have the same validity as *a priori* relations of ideas. To clarify this proposition, Hume famously offers the following famous example: "*That the sun will not rise tomorrow* is no less intelligible a proposition, and implies no more contradiction, than the affirmation, *that it will rise*. We should in vain, therefore, attempt to demonstrate its falsehood" (*Enquiries*, 25–26). Whereas logical claims are by definition true, inferences about cause and effect relations based on empirical observation are only probably true. The fact that the sun rose every day for millennia does not guarantee that it will rise in the future—it only makes it highly probable that it will do so. Consequently, we could claim that empirical statements are the dialectical opposites of logical or analytical statements. While analytical statements yield objective and certain knowledge, empirical statements do not. This chain of reasoning leads Hume to the controversial conclusion that humans cannot attain certain knowledge of the external world.

As the example of the sun rising indicates, "All reasonings concerning matter of fact seem to be founded on the relation of *Cause and Effect*. By means of that relation alone we can go beyond the evidence of our memory and senses" (*Enquiries*, 26). Hume provides two further thought experiments to undermine confidence in causal reasoning. In the first example, he asks readers to imagine that "A man finding a watch or any other machine in a desert island, would conclude that there had once been men in that island. All our reasonings concerning fact are of the same nature. And here it is constantly supposed that there is a connexion between the present fact and that which is inferred from it" (*Enquiries*, 26–27). Hume's point is not that the man finding a man-made object is wrong to infer that other humans are present on the island, but that this inference cannot be proven to be correct. The same can be said, Hume adds, about the supposed rational truth-certainty and constancy of the Newtonian laws of nature:

> But to convince us that all the laws of nature, and all the operations of bodies without exception, are known only by experience, the following reflections may, perhaps, suffice. . . . The mind can never possibly find the effect in the supposed cause, by the most accurate scrutiny and examination. . . . A stone or piece of metal raised into the air, and left without any support, immediately falls: but to consider the matter *a priori*, is there anything we discover in this situation which can beget the idea of a downward, rather than upward, or any other motion, in the stone or metal? (*Enquiries*, 28)

Hume's examples can be interpreted in two ways. First, the philosopher may be implying that the laws of nature, including Newton's law of gravity, which postulates that gravity is inversely proportional to the square distance between two masses, are subject to change as our observations of nature improve. Our scientific tools and accumulated knowledge may reveal that the law of gravity is only approximately and locally correct, as has been shown by Einstein's theory of relativity. This objection does not fundamentally undermine the objective and rational foundation of empirical knowledge: it only suggests that it is subject to verification and improvement. A more plausible interpretation of Hume's example, however, suggests that the laws of nature themselves can radically change or that humans cannot know if their empirical knowledge is true. According to Hume, there is no guarantee that gravity will always work the same way. Newton himself extrapolated the law of gravity based upon how gravity seems to work; that, however, may change or be altogether inaccurate. What leads us then to infer that the sun will rise tomorrow? Not objective reasoning, answers Hume, but habit or custom. "All inferences from experience," he concludes, "therefore, are effects of custom, not of reasoning. Custom, then, is the great guide of human life. It is that principle alone which renders our experience useful to us, and makes us expect, for the future, a similar train of events with those which have appeared in the past" (*Enquiries*, 43–44). By means of a single dialectical process that negates the certainty of sensory perception, Hume arrives at a skepticist subjectivism, which postulates that humans cannot be certain of the accuracy of our empirical knowledge. The lack of objectivity, however, does not lead Hume to espouse full-fledged relativism. After all, the inference that the future will resemble the past is not arbitrary, but based on high probabilities rather than the truth-certainty assumed by objectivist rationalists. In his subjectivist skepticism, Hume aims to expose the "narrow limits of human reason and capacity" while at the same time not abandoning the search for truth.

Hume takes great pains to distinguish his "moderate skepticism" from dogmatic relativism. His skepticism, he claims, "may be understood in a very reasonable sense, and is a necessary preparative to the study of philosophy, by preserving a proper impartiality in our judgments, and weaning our mind from all those prejudices, which we may have imbibed from education or rash opinion" (*Enquiries*, 150). Like his philosophical precursors and opponents, Hume proposes that to discover true knowledge, philosophers must "begin with clear and self-evident principles, to advance by timorous and sure steps, to review frequently our conclusions, and examine accurately all their consequences" (*Enquiries*, 150). The problem for Hume, as for Kant, would remain: what are those clear and self-evident principles? If humans cannot be certain that the reality they perceive is true and unchanging, then what is left of human knowledge?

Kant's Response to Hume's Skepticism: The Transcendental Deduction

Kant proposes to address precisely this question. Provoked by Hume's skepticism, he declares:

> Since the essays of Locke and Leibnitz, or rather since the origin of metaphysics so far as we know its history, nothing has ever happened which could have been more decisive to its fate than the attack made upon it by David Hume. He threw no light on this kind of knowledge; but he certainly struck a spark from which light might have been obtained, had it caught some flammable substance and had its smouldering fire been carefully nursed and developed.[10] (*Prolegomena*, 3)

Hume's challenge to objectivism induces Kant to create a new epistemology that mediates between subjectivism and objectivism.[11] The essential question for epistemology, Kant maintains, is how can knowledge be both only anthropocentric—or filtered by a human perspective and constrained by its limitations—and at the same time objectively true. In the preface to the first edition of the *Critique*, Kant answers this question by suggesting that there are two kinds of relations between knower and object of knowledge—one delineated by empiricism, the other by idealism: "There are only two possible ways in which synthetic representations and their objects can establish connection, obtain necessary relation to one another, and, as it were, meet one another. Either the object alone must make the representation possible, or the representation alone must make the object possible" (124). Idealism and empiricism, Kant explains, are intertwined in what can be described as a single dialectical, and thus mutually exclusive, relation:

> In the former case, this relation is only empirical, and the representation is never possible *a priori*. This is true of appearances, as regards that [element] in them which belongs to sensation. In the latter case, representation in itself does not produce its object in so far as *existence* is concerned, for we are not here speaking of its causality by means of the will. (124)

If we accept Hume's empiricist hypothesis, we are led to the conclusion that our perception of external reality has little or nothing to do with our *a priori* faculties. In other words, empiricism minimizes (or negates) the influence of analytic faculties to argue that human reality is principally determined by external objects. Idealism, however, begins from the opposite assumption. It posits that the source of knowledge is human imagination rather than external reality. Described in terms of the logic of the dialectic, idealism minimizes (or negates) the influence of the external world upon human perception. Both epistemologies, Kant suggests, are partly correct and partly incorrect. External reality, he maintains, affects perception, but human faculties in turn determine our conception of reality:

> Now all experience does indeed contain, in addition to the intuition of the senses through which something is given, a *concept* of an object as being thereby given, that is to say, as appearing. Concepts of objects in general thus underlie all empirical knowledge as its *a priori* conditions. The objective

validity of the categories as *a priori* concepts rests, therefore, on the fact that, so far as the form of thought is concerned, through them alone does experience become possible. They relate of necessity and *a priori* to objects of experience, for the reason that only by means of them can any object whatsoever of experience be thought. (124–25)

Hume and Berkeley were misguided in defining knowledge in terms of a mutually exclusive binary hierarchy. Empiricism underestimates the function of human imagination, while idealism denies the influence of the external world upon human perception. Without our *a priori* analytical capacities, Kant argues, we could not conceptualize objects of perception. At the same time, without the existence of external objects, we would have nothing to conceptualize.[12] Kant uses rationalist insights to critique empiricism and empiricist insights to critique rationalism. All knowledge begins with experience as empiricists maintain; but our *a priori* understanding (the categories) give us the sense of time, space, and other concepts that shape experience. On the one hand, Kant agrees with Hume that sensory perception may not give us true knowledge of the laws of nature. On the other hand, he also agrees with Leibnitz that the laws of nature are universal and cannot change from day to day. Knowledge is transcendental, Kant states, because it depends upon our apperception of things-in-themselves, which he calls "noumena." At the same time, knowledge is idealist because the external world is (in part) a product of reason.

To account for the possible interaction between human faculties and the external world, Kant advances a new concept called "the categories." The categories decode the external world in a way that somehow corresponds to our innate *a priori* conceptions, including the notions of shape, quantity, and time. The difficult task left for Kant is to explain the manner in which the categories can perform this sublation between human perception (phenomena) and true reality (noumena). The philosopher addresses this problem directly in one of the most important sections of the *Critique*, entitled "The Transcendental Deduction."

In this chapter, Kant combines aspects of empiricism and idealism—and introduces his unique concepts—to produce transcendental idealism, which, as noted, posits that the world of experience depends upon the activity of reason. "The transcendental deduction of all *a priori* concepts," Kant explains, "has thus a principle according to which the whole enquiry must be directed, namely, that they must be recognised as *a priori* conditions of the possibility of experience, whether of the intuition which is to be met within it or of the thought" (126). Kant attempts to demonstrate that the order and regularity of nature, understood as the sum of our experiences, is determined by the subjective conditions of the understanding. That is to say, our conception of the external world is the result of the understanding's application of pure *a priori* concepts, or categories, to appearances. Because the categories constitute the formal conditions of all experience, there can be no experience of an object that is not subject to them.

As Kant elaborates, "the order and regularity in the appearances, which we entitle *nature*, we ourselves introduce. We could never find them in appearances, had not we ourselves, or the nature of our mind, originally set them there" (147). By means of this correlation, the philosopher aims to resolve the epistemological conflict between external world and subjective conception. Internal experience is not opposed to external reality, as both idealism and empiricism postulate. Rather, human understanding simultaneously incorporates and negates aspects of external reality. According to Kant, "Sensibility gives us forms (of intuition), but understanding gives us rules" (147). How can we know that the rules provided by our subjective understanding are objectively true? "The latter [i.e., understanding]," Kant suggests, "is always occupied in investigating appearances, in order to detect some rule in them. Rules, so far as they are objective, and therefore necessarily depend upon the knowledge of the object, are called laws" (147). Having combined aspects of empiricism and idealism, Kant performs the same dialectical sublation of subjectivism and objectivism.

To resolve the opposition between subjectivism and objectivism, which he believes leads either to an epistemological impasse or to dogmatism, Kant maintains: "Although we learn many laws through experience, they are only special determinations of still higher laws, and the highest of these, under which the others all stand, issue *a priori* from the understanding itself" (147). The categories thus represent a mediating structure—both subjective and objective, both empirical and rational—that makes shared and orderly perception of the world possible. Subjectivism, as we recall, claims that all knowledge is a matter of personal or anthropocentric perspective, and thus that its truth-certainty or validity cannot be established. By way of contrast, objectivism claims that all knowledge results from the regularity of the laws of nature, laws which we can extrapolate through observation and reasoning. Kant crosses chiasmically the connotations of skepticist subjectivism and rationalist

CHAPTER TWO

objectivism by selectively incorporating and negating aspects of the two theories. He integrates Hume's skeptical subjectivism into his theory by accepting the assumption that humans cannot be certain of the accuracy of their empirical observations and of the constancy of the laws of nature. He rejects, or negates, however, the skepticist conclusion that humans have no access to true knowledge of the world. Simultaneously, Kant incorporates aspects of rationalist objectivism by arguing that we can be certain of the accuracy and regularity of human conceptions of the world. He maintains, however, that human faculties, rather than the laws of nature, determine the regularity of our experience. Ordered sensory impressions "are not borrowed from experience; on the contrary, they have to confer upon appearances their conformity to law, and so to make experience possible" (147). Consequently, Kant concludes, the subjective conceptions of the world provided by the categories make possible what we call objective knowledge; while conversely, our so-called objective knowledge may be nothing more than inference based on custom, as Hume claimed.

In observing a dialectical logic that inverts the traditional connotations of objectivism and subjectivism, however, transcendental idealism creates its own counterintuitive opposition between objectivity and subjectivity. This new epistemology gives subjectivism the status formerly assumed by objectivism:

> Thus the understanding is something more than a power of formulating rules through comparison of appearances; it is itself the lawgiver of nature. Save through it, nature, that is, synthetic unity of the manifold of appearances according to rules, would not exist at all (for appearances, as such, cannot exist outside us—they exist only in our sensibility). (147)

Experiences are not based upon the independent laws of nature, Kant maintains. Rather, we experience an object only when the understanding applies a category of judgment to the synthesis of a manifold. Through this function of the understanding, nature, which is the sum total of our experiences, conforms to subjective conditions. The question remains: having performed a sublation between objectivism and subjectivism and between empiricism and rationalism, has Kant solved the problem of truth-certainty? How does he demonstrate the validity and accuracy of our subjective conceptions of the world?

To address this question, Kant begins with the assumption that skepticism is disproved by the fact that we have synthetic *a priori* knowledge of "pure mathematics and general science of nature" (128). Rather than being concerned with whether or not we attain certain knowledge, Kant investigates the grounds for its existence. Nonetheless, we are led to ask: has transcendental idealism provided a satisfactory refutation of the claims that we cannot have synthetic *a priori* knowledge and that nature operates according to laws which are independent of our minds? Perhaps mathematical judgments are purely analytic, and thus *a priori* knowledge of them has no implications for our knowledge of the empirical world. The claim that we have *a priori* synthetic knowledge of the general science of nature begs the question. It is worthwhile, then, to assess the claims of the transcendental deduction from the perspective that we might not have synthetic *a priori* knowledge, to see if this theory can account for it.

Let us first examine the relation of the understanding to nature. Kant believes that we may not know "things-in-themselves" (noumena).[13] Our understanding deals only with appearances (phenomena), and nature is simply "the order and regularity in . . . appearances" (112). Appearances, in turn, exist only insofar as they appear to a subject. Consequently, Kant reasons, one cannot speak of laws of nature that exist independently of the understanding. If independent laws do not exist, it follows that "we ourselves introduce" the apparent order and regularity of nature. The process by which we introduce the laws of nature, Kant observes, begins "with what must first be given," namely, the intuition of a manifold. (112) A manifold, which constitutes the abstract impression that is the blueprint of human knowledge, can be intuited only in accordance with pure forms of sensibility such as space and time. Once intuited, a manifold is then combined with consciousness to form a perception, which is subsequently synthesized by the imagination in an act called apprehension. As Kant elaborates:

> What is first given to us is appearance. When combined with consciousness, it is called perception. . . . Now, since every appearance contains a manifold, and since different perceptions therefore occur in the mind separately and singly, a combination of them, such as they cannot have in sense itself, is demanded. There must therefore exist in us an active faculty for the synthesis of this manifold. To this faculty I give the title, imagination. Its action, when immediately directed upon perceptions, I entitle apprehension. . . .
>
> But it is clear that even this apprehension of the manifold would not by itself produce an image and a connection of the impressions, were it not that there exists a subjective ground which leads the mind to reinstate a preceding perception alongside the subsequent perception to which it has passed, and

so to form whole series of perceptions. This is the reproductive faculty of
imagination, which is merely empirical. (143–44)

A synthesis of an intuited manifold is required because all experience must conform to the condition of the unity of consciousness.[14] Without such unity, we would not have experiences as a single being. That is to say, we would not be able to attach the "I think" (*cogito*) to all of our representations. Comprehensible experience becomes possible only when the understanding applies a category to an appearance which has been synthesized by the imagination. This act, Kant argues, represents the process of making a judgment. A judgment, in turn, consists of bringing a manifold under the condition of the unity of consciousness.

The categories, Kant further postulates, represent forms of judgment. They provide the rules for connecting, or synthesizing, appearances into unified concepts so that they can appear to the understanding under the condition of the unity of consciousness. The unification of a manifold into a concept is clearly a synthetic act, which is to say, an act of the mind upon appearances. Consequently, the rules governing this act are not to be found objectively, or independently of the mind in nature. Instead, knowledge of nature depends upon our subjective faculties. Nature, understood as the order and regularity of appearances, results from our faculty of bringing "the synthesis of a manifold . . . to the unity of apperception" (161). Apart from this subjective thinking process, Kant maintains, the external world has no knowable existence.

From this brief account of Kant's epistemology, it might appear that the philosopher has provided a satisfactory refutation of the objectivist claim that nature, understood as the sum of our experiences, operates according to laws independent of our minds. In arriving at this conclusion, Kant seems to employ a dialectical logic that refutes (or negates) rationalist objectivism. In so doing, he also seems to arrive at a subjectivist position, or, at any rate, at a skeptical conception of knowledge. But this is not the case. Having negated rationalist objectivism, Kant proceeds to negate subjectivism. To see if Kant's epistemology successfully incorporates and negates both objectivism and subjectivism, we must follow the second loop of his double dialectical process, which attempts to establish the objectivity of subjective knowledge.

In evaluating this turn in his argument, I will show that there is an important omission in Kant's epistemology, which weakens his theory. Kant does not describe the origins of the intuited manifolds that are synthesized into our experiences. Instead, he dismisses the origin of manifolds as an unimportant issue. "Whatever the origin of our representations," he contends, "whether they are due to the influence of outer things, or are produced through inner causes, whether they arise *a priori*, or being appearances have an empirical origin . . ." leads to the conclusion that human representations of the world are true. (131) Such speculation suggests that the particular origin of a manifold is either unimportant or indeterminate and need not be addressed. This omission is crucial because it is difficult to support the claim that the understanding imposes order and regularity upon nature without reference to the effect of the manifold upon intuition. Let me explain.

It seems that the understanding deserves credit for introducing the order and regularity of appearances only insofar as the intuited manifolds which give rise to appearances are themselves disorderly and irregular. If manifolds are received in sequence, however, and if each manifold leads to a particular concept according to this sequence, it cannot be the case that intuited manifolds are any less orderly or regular than appearances. Given that a particular manifold is synthesized into a concept according to definite rules provided by the categories, it follows that this same manifold, whenever intuited, produces the same concept. Furthermore, given that concepts arise in our minds according to the order in which we intuit manifolds, it follows that the sequence of the intuitions of manifolds must be as ordered and regular as the experiences which arise when the understanding synthesizes the manifolds. Moreover, if the order of reception of these manifolds determines the order of the concepts of experience, it follows that the faculty of understanding is not the lawgiver of nature, but only the translator of disconnected but regular manifolds into connected empirical concepts. The regularity of appearances must derive ultimately from manifolds that are equally regular, because any irregularity in a manifold would result in an irregularity in appearances. Consequently, we are led to the conclusion that the understanding serves no other function than to render manifolds presentable. The understanding translates the manifolds into forms that can be comprehended by the "I of apperception," in the same sense that one might translate German into English.

This translation must, of course, proceed according to definite rules, which may be provided by the categories. The application of these categories to manifolds of appearance, however, no more introduces the regularity of those manifolds than the application of the rules of translation into English renders a German text more regular. That is to say, if cognition is understood as the process of intuiting manifolds in a certain order (rather than simultaneously) and of forming concepts from these manifolds as they are intuited, one cannot attribute the order and regularity of nature to the understanding. The blueprint for this order has been provided along with the intuited manifold of appearances. One must therefore look to this manifold for the origin of that order which we see reflected in the world around us. This deduction, in turn, raises the question: how is it that the manifold of appearances that is given to our sensibility contains the seeds for the laws of nature?

It must be the case that the source of these manifolds is also the source of the order and regularity of the natural world. Three possibilities for the source of the manifolds immediately present themselves: the self, God, and things-in-themselves. If a faculty of the self (such as the imagination) produces the manifolds we intuit, then we have a self-contained system which renders shared experience impossible without reference to a principle that unifies the productive faculties of all human beings. The concept of God might serve as such a principle, as it does in Berkeley's idealism. In this case, however, God, and not the understanding, functions as the lawgiver of nature. Finally, the claim that it is a fact of human nature that our experiences can be shared even though there is no independent objective reality, might also serve as a unifying principle. It is doubtful, however, that Kant suggests either of these two possibilities as the source of our intuitions. He indicates that intuitions ultimately originate from something that is distinct from the self. In addition, the concept of God does not play an important role in this part of his epistemology.

The third possibility, namely, that the manifolds are somehow produced by things-in-themselves, corresponds more closely to Kant's theory. In the preface to the second edition, the philosopher speculates: "though we cannot *know* these objects as things in themselves, we must yet be in position at least to *think* them as things-in-themselves; otherwise we should be landed in the absurd conclusion that there can be appearance without anything that appears" (27). If we accept that things-in-themselves provide the manifold of appearances which our minds synthesize into experience, and that concepts arise according to definite rules and in accordance with these manifolds, we are led to the inevitable conclusion that things-in-themselves are the lawgivers of nature. The order and regularity of nature—that is, our experiences—must be completely derived from the order of intuited manifolds, and therefore ultimately from what gives us the manifold—namely, things-in-themselves.

Such a traditionally objectivist conclusion obviously runs contrary to Kant's transcendental idealism. In other words, by following the second loop of the dialectic and negating skepticism, Kant's theory reverts into the rationalist objectivism that it also attempts to refute.

One way to address this problem is to assert that the understanding's contribution to synthesizing a manifold is so substantial that it overshadows the particular characteristics of that manifold on which the unique identity of the concept is based. For example, although it must be the case that only a certain manifold will be synthesized into the concept "dog," one cannot say that the experience of the dog is derived from this manifold because the manifold is too dissimilar from the concept. According to this interpretation, the understanding determines for itself how to synthesize a particular manifold, even though it does so by means of set rules. This explanation, however, does not adequately address the objection that the order and regularity of human experience must ultimately be derived from the source of our intuitions. It remains the case that a given manifold, upon intuition, necessarily leads to a particular concept, and thus contains the distinctive features that determine that concept.

Another way to address this problem is to assert that our minds selectively intuit only those appearances that conform to order and regularity, even though the world from which we get these intuitions is itself chaotic and amorphous. Thus our faculty of intuition is somehow limited to that which is ordered, and in effect we cull order from chaos. It remains unclear, however, how the faculty of intuition can discern only that which is ordered, when there can be no order in chaos. It would seem that even if we are limited by our senses to certain forms of intuition—such as light within the visible spectrum or sound above a minimum decibel level—such sensory impressions cannot appear as ordered and regular if they originate from chaos unless the faculty of intuition somehow stores the manifolds it randomly receives until it has sufficient material to form a coherent experience. In any case, the understanding plays no role in the ordering of appearances other than preparing them for experience by making them conform to the conditions of the unity of consciousness. According to this interpretation of Kant's epistemology, the order and regularity of appearances as we experience them can be traced to our faculty of intuition. This faculty precedes the understanding, and accordingly the understanding is not the lawgiver of nature.

Yet another attempt to solve this problem, which I believe is closer to the Kantian position, would be to argue that the order of intuitions does not determine the order of concepts of experience. That is to say, the fact that we intuit one manifold before another does not mean that the manifold gives rise to a particular concept before another. Instead, the understanding produces order out of amorphous intuition. We intuit various garbled manifolds which follow no rhyme or reason. Subsequently, the understanding selects those intuitions which can be part of an ordered experience. The understanding then stores those manifolds that it randomly receives until it forms a coherent experience, or else it culls from amorphous intuition those intuitions necessary for creating a coherent experience. Indeed, it seems that Kant makes such an argument when he proclaims, "we could never find [order and regularity] in appearances, had not we ourselves, or the nature of our mind, originally set them there" (147). Accepting this proposition, which is closer to subjectivism than to objectivism, we encounter an additional difficulty.

If each of our individual understandings searches among amorphous intuitions for those intuitions which conform to an ordered experience, how can we explain the fact that we experience the world as though it had an objective existence for all individuals? That is to say, what unifies experience of the same phenomenon so that two people in a given location will have experiences that more or less correspond to those they would have if their environment existed independently of either of their minds? How is it that human experience, which according to Kant exists only in our minds, seems to relate to a nature that exists independently of our minds? Clearly some sort of unifying principle is necessary to explain similar experiences of (what appears to be) the same incident. When two people are in the same setting, it is generally the case that, for instance, when one sees the sun set or hears a whistle blow, so does the other. What explains this similar experience? Kant maintains that it cannot be the case that the light of the sun or sound exists independently of human minds, because experience is a function of the understanding. Furthermore, because intuitions are amorphous, it cannot be the case that their source generates this seemingly independent objectivity which makes possible shared experience.

Once again, according to Kantian epistemology, things-in-themselves (noumena) cannot be the objective standard that gives us the sense of shared experience. It may be that God ensures that everything we experience corresponds to what we would experience if there were a physical world independent of our minds. Kant, however, does not subscribe to this view. The only real candidate for a unifying principle seems to be human nature. Our imaginations are so composed that we all have experiences as though there were an objective reality existing independently of our minds and determining the order and regularity of our impressions, even though, in fact, we ourselves introduce such order and regularity. This chain of reasoning, which negates rationalist objectivism, nonetheless remains trapped in both the idealism and the skepticism that it attempts to (also) undo. Kant has not fully succeeded in demonstrating the objective validity of subjective knowledge. Unless he can do so, however, he reaches the conventionally idealist position that reality is a product of the human mind, one of the two positions that he was attempting to refute. In other words, Kant still needs to demonstrate how knowledge is both transcendental and idealist.

Although Kant's idealist hypothesis is no more refutable than Descartes's brain-in-a-vat thought experiment, it can be challenged for a similar reason—it is a less elegant explanation of experience than its converse, namely, that an independent nature determines, at least in part, the laws which govern appearances. Kant's conception of human imagination assumes that our minds universally and necessarily ascribe order and regularity to experience. In so doing, it does not lend any more necessity or universality to human experience than does a realist perspective that assumes that human perceptions can provide knowledge of a mind-independent reality. After all, Kant does not assert that all laws of nature are valid *a priori*, or that nature must appear to us exactly as it does. He only claims that experience must conform to a range of conditions. Within these conditions, experience is not fully determined. As he observes, "Special laws, as concerning those appearances which are empirically determined, cannot in their specific character be *derived* from the categories, although they are one and all subject to them" (173). Consequently, we can conclude that there must be some ground for the seeming objectivity of shared experience other than the claim that "special laws" are a necessary precondition for having the experience.

To say that the seemingly independent objectivity of the order of nature is not, at least in part, a necessary precondition for having coherent experience, raises the question of how a particular experience whose order cannot be derived from the categories seems to apply nonetheless to individuals as though it had an objective, independent existence. Assuming that one cannot derive from the categories specific information—such as that in a certain wing of a certain museum there is a certain painting—how are we to account for the fact that this painting can be seen by more than one person? That is to say, if shared experience is too specific to be explained by reference to human nature, it cannot be done by reference to the categories. Thus the order and regularity of experience is based upon what amounts to the axiom that human beings, as a result of their nature, have experiences as though there were an independent objective reality which determined them, even though there is not. Given these considerations, it is more plausible to assert that the reason that ordered and regular experiences seem to have objective validity for a group of people is because they are determined by the order and regularity of an external nature that they perceive.

If we accept the proposition that the understanding is the lawgiver of nature, then the order and regularity of experience cannot be based upon any organization inherent in manifolds upon intuition. Yet if this is the case, then we must explain the phenomenon of shared experience, that is, the seemingly independent objectivity of the material world. This is not accomplished by the transcendental deduction, which posits that experience must conform to the understanding in some respects, but certainly not in all respects. Skepticism remains a plausible theory for those who reject the idea that we have the sort of knowledge Kant ascribes to us, and for those to whom the question of which theory more efficiently describes the world as we experience holds paramount importance.

I raise this objection because the assertion that nature conforms to the conditions of the mind is not self-evident. We could easily perform a more intuitive sublation of subjectivism and objectivism. We might suppose, for instance, incorporating aspects of rationalist objectivism, that nature operates according to laws that determine our experience. We might also suppose, incorporating aspects of skepticist subjectivism, that we cannot have absolute knowledge of nature, because we can never know for certain that the tendencies we have observed in the past will continue in the future. This double dialectical selective incorporation and negation of both objectivism and subjectivism—which, unlike the single dialectic, acknowledges the strengths of both theories—leads to an epistemology of partial knowledge. Such an epistemology supports the commonsense assumption that human beings have some knowledge of the external world, which operates in accordance with natural laws, but concedes that we cannot be absolutely certain of its accuracy. As we shall see in subsequent chapters, this anthropocentric realism—which, according to my interpretation, is the product of the double dialectical sublation of both objectivism and subjectivism—would later be developed not only by Enlightenment philosophes such as d'Alembert, but also by contemporary epistemologists such as Roy Bhaskar.

Notes

1. I will be citing, once again, from Norman Kemp Smith's translation of Kant's *Critique of Pure Reason*.
2. I would like to thank Dan Troyka for his significant and thoughtful contributions to this essay.
3. In *Kant's Transcendental Idealism: An Interpretation and Defense*, Henry Allison argues that the central elements of Kant's epistemology—namely that we perceive reality as it really is and that noumena, or things-in-themselves, exist objectively and permanently as opposed to changing in space and time—are conclusions which are assumed from the beginning of the argument rather than proven logically.
4. Van Cleeve, *Problems from Kant*, 4.
5. See Arthur W. Collins's *Possible Experience: Understanding Kant's Critique of Pure Reason*.
6. See Graham Bird's *Kant's Theory of Knowledge: An Outline of One Central Argument in the* Critique of Pure Reason. As Bird observes, "The problem is that of explaining the relation of appearances to categories" (59).
7. See H. W. Cassirer's *Kant's First Critique: An Appraisal of the Permanent Significance of Kant's* Critique of Pure Reason.
8. As Paul Guyer argues in the *Introduction to The Cambridge Companion to Kant*, "For Kant, then, his profound recognition of our legislative power in both science and morals, in both theoretical and practical reason, always had to be reconciled with an equally deep sense of the contingency of our success in both theory and practice. . . . After he wrote, no one could ever again think of either science or morality as a matter of the passive reception of entirely external truth or reality. In reflection upon the methods of science as well as in many particular areas of science itself, the recognition of our own input into the world we claim to know has become inescapable" (2–3). For a more lengthy analysis of Kant's mediation between objectivism and subjectivism, see also Guyer's *Kant and the Claims of Knowledge*.
9. I will be citing the Oxford reprint of the 1777 edition of Hume's *Enquiries Concerning Human Understanding and Concerning the Principles of Morals*.
10. Kant, *Prolegomena to Any Future Metaphysic*, 3.
11. For book-length analyses of (primarily) the transcendental deduction, see J. N. Findlay's *Kant and the Transcendental Object: A Hermeneutic Study*, Henry E. Allison's *Kant's Transcendental Idealism* and Richard E. Aquila's *Matter in Mind: A Study of Kant's Transcendental Deduction*.

CHAPTER TWO

12. For discussions of how Kant critiques former paradigms of reason, see Frederick C. Beiser's *The Fate of Reason: German Philosophy from Kant to Fichte* and Onora O'Neill's *Constructions of Reason: Explorations of Kant's Practical Philosophy*.

13. Kant makes contradictory statements about whether or not humans have access to the noumena, and hence to things-in-themselves. Consequently, critics disagree about this fundamental aspect of Kantian philosophy.

14. For a detailed explanation of Kant's model of the unity of consciousness, see Hubert Shwyzer's *The Unity of Understanding*.

CHAPTER THREE

Beyond the Particular and the Universal: D'Alembert's "Discours préliminaire" to the *Encyclopédie*

In academic circles, the debate between universalists and relativists seems to be as lively today as it was during the Enlightenment, when Denis Diderot and Jean Le Rond d'Alembert debated the nature of truth.[1] Although we may be relying upon Enlightenment philosophy to conduct our own debates about knowledge, the terms of discussion have become more polarized today than they were during the eighteenth century. This essay argues that an important element, namely the middle ground between universalism and relativism, has been left out of contemporary reformulations of Enlightenment thought. Both relativist and universalist theories adopt what I call a single dialectical epistemology.[2] According to this paradigm, true knowledge represents the elimination (or negation) of every source of error, social bias, or personal perspective. By way of contrast, I will demonstrate that Enlightenment thought, and particularly d'Alembert's "Discours préliminaire,"[3] elaborates a more nuanced, double dialectical, theory of knowledge. As I will explain, a double dialectical process combines the quest for truth with an awareness of human differences and limitations. Let me indicate briefly how contemporary criticism has reduced Enlightenment epistemology to a single dialectical relation between truth and error and, consequently, why we need to reconsider Enlightenment epistemology.

On the one hand, objectivist theories claim that the producers of knowledge have the cognitive ability to describe the universe as it really is, not only as they perceive it to be from either a subjective or an anthropocentric perspective. Objectivist epistemologies thus imply that the producers of knowledge are (or could become) unbiased in their quest for truth. Such theories also assume that rational individuals share a transhistorical, permanent set of standards that enables them to convey information. Objectivist epistemologies are consequently also universalist because they posit one true way of perceiving the world.

Jürgen Habermas's theorization of communicative action represents one of the most noteworthy scholarly efforts to defend the universalist legacy of the Enlightenment. To establish the validity of empirical and rational knowledge, Habermas observes a single dialectical process. In *The Theory of Communicative Action*,[4] he maintains that "A judgment can be objective if it is undertaken on the basis of a *transsubjective* validity claim that has the same meaning for observers and nonparticipants as it has for the acting subject himself" (9). I call Habermas's definition of truth "single dialectical" because the critic represents knowledge as the result of a process of selective negation and incorporation. To reach a transsubjective consensus about the content of truth and the process of acquiring knowledge, a person or community must eliminate all sources of error—such as personal bias, emotional investment, and selfish interests—while at the same time incorporating those methods or facts which have stood the test of time.

Universalist scholarship such as that of Habermas not only seeks to preserve the universalist legacy of the Enlightenment. It also reacts against the perceived threat posed by cotemporary scholarly movements that attempt to refute universalism and retrieve the particularist tendencies of Enlightenment thought.[5] Influential critics such as Michel Foucault and Jean-François Lyotard attribute the notions of truth and falsehood to relations of power rather than to objective standards of validity. Relativist theories assert that there are practically an infinite number of acceptable ways of acquiring information. Although some forms of knowledge may gain more cultural value than others, no form of knowledge is demonstrably superior to others.

Foucault has been one of the most sophisticated critics of universalist Enlightenment epistemology and its contemporary legacy. Nonetheless, I would argue that his theory of knowledge also relies upon a single dialectical model. Like Habermas, Foucault defines truth as the negation of human bias and error. In the famous chapter "Man and His Doubles" in *The Order of Things*,[6] Foucault comments upon the apparent paradox of the human condition. On the one hand, he states, humans aspire to objective knowledge. On the other hand, he adds, we remain trapped in a human body and mind that reduce our quest for absolute truth to a limited and fragile knowledge:

> Man, in the analytic of finitude, is a strange empirico-transcendental doublet, since he is a being such that knowledge will be attained in him of what renders all knowledge possible. . . . For the threshold of our modernity is situated not by the attempt to apply objective methods to the study of man, but rather by the constitution of an empirico-transcendental doublet which was called man. (*The Order of Things*, 318–19)

If knowledge is defined in terms of a single dialectical process that eliminates all limitations, biases and errors, then Foucault is correct to state that man is trapped in a double bind. According to the logic of the single dialectic, to attain truth, we are compelled to project a superhuman subject: either by means of the transsubjective communication that eventually leads to universally valid claims (as suggested by Habermas) or by means of the metaphysical projections (be they religious, social, or scientific) critiqued by Foucault. While Habermas finds the multiplication of perspectives a path to objective truth (to a more comprehensive unity, consensus), Foucault ultimately rejects the impossible division of the human subject and lapses into relativism. If humans cannot transcend their anthropocentric limitations, he reasons, then no true knowledge is possible.

What is wrong with the present opposition between objectivism and relativism? Along with critics such as Richard Bernstein, who aim to find a path in between relativism and objectivism, I believe that if we accept either universalist or particularist epistemology, we have little hope of answering the most perplexing questions about human existence.[7] In their crudest form, universalist theories of knowledge permit no genuine debates about truth-claims. The assertion that a given statement is—or should be regarded as—universally true reduces all disagreements to errors or misjudgments. Conversely—but equally dangerous for the pursuit of knowledge—relativist theories render not only the search for truth but also the transmission of information itself meaningless. If all truth claims were indeed nothing but a series of competing language games, then the notion of validity would be either reduced to relations of domination—where one regime of truth unjustifiably reigns over others—or transformed into inconsequential and sophistical verbal exchanges. Relativism thus eliminates all efforts to present rational, or even acceptable, justifications for statements, beliefs, and actions. A good theory of knowledge, I believe, must avoid both of these extremes while also incorporating their useful elements. On the one hand, like universalist theories, it should enable critics to distinguish valid from invalid statements and to offer good

CHAPTER THREE

justifications for such distinctions. On the other hand, like relativist theories, it should incorporate a multiplicity of perspectives and acknowledge human limitations.

In the "Discours préliminaire," d'Alembert proposes such a theory of knowledge by outlining a dialectical process that combines aspects of universalism and particularism while ultimately overcoming both. By way of contrast to objectivists, d'Alembert does not believe that humans can attain unmediated knowledge. At the same time, unlike relativists, he does not give up the quest for (local) truths:

> Far from wishing to obscure a truth which is recognized and undisputed even by skeptics, let us leave it up to enlightened metaphysicians to develop its principle. It is up to them to determine, if possible, which progression the soul observes in its first step beyond itself, as it is pushed, so to speak, and at the same time restrained by a host of perceptions which, on the one hand, propel it toward external objects, and on the other hand, belonging only to the soul, seem to circumscribe for it a narrow space from which they do not allow it to escape. (ii)

How can humans know that the reality they perceive is objectively true? To answer this question, d'Alembert first dismisses as disingenuous the type of skepticism that casts doubt upon all human knowledge. After negating skepticism, d'Alembert proceeds to negate objectivism. According to d'Alembert, the question of whether our anthropocentric knowledge is objectively true is an unanswerable question. As Foucault would later argue, humans cannot step outside of themselves to verify the accuracy of our perception. Human knowledge, d'Alembert suggests, occupies a space between complete certainty and doubt. To overcome the impasse between relativism and objectivism, d'Alembert doubles the single dialectical process that structures this opposition. He envisions a new relationship between truth and error which, borrowing Luce Irigaray's terminology, I will call a "chiasmus" or a "double dialectics."[8] Let me now explain how a double dialectical process operates and how it improves upon a single dialectical epistemology.

As we have seen, in a single dialectical relationship the concepts of universalism and relativism are created by means of a process of mutual negation. Once trapped in this single dialectical opposition, philosophers are faced with the unpalatable option of choosing either relativism or universalism. By way of contrast, reading these concepts in terms of a double dialectics would suggest that the categories of particularity and difference are not only semantically interrelated, but also inseparable. By depending upon the negation of particularities, the category of the universal simultaneously incorporates the concept of the particular. The same logic applies to the semiotic formation of the particular by means of the negation of the universal. The twin goals of achieving a pure universal by eliminating all particulars or, conversely, of celebrating only differences by negating the universal are unachievable according to the logic of any dialectical process, be it Hegelian or chiasmic.

There is one major difference, however, between the single and the double dialectics. The single dialectic creates a binary hierarchy where *only* one term acquires value by negating the value of the other. Universalists create "objective knowledge" by eliminating all subjective circumstances and opinions. Likewise, relativists produce subjective knowledge by dismissing the possibility of founded agreement. By way of contrast, the double dialectics enables both interrelated terms—the particular and the universal—to attain what I would call "positive identity." By a "positive identity" I mean that both terms are defined through the simultaneous incorporation and negation of the other term. When the universal and the particular are produced by means of a single dialectical process that privileges only one term and excludes the other, there is no real possibility for open-ended but nonrelativistic theories of knowledge. Only when both particularist and universalist claims are granted an equivalent value can we hope to arrive at a philosophical scheme that overcomes the hierarchical dichotomy of universalism and particularism without renouncing either category. Without an appreciation of the notion of difference as essential to the notion of sameness—meaning not only as essential to its definition but also to its critique—we cannot avoid epistemological and ethical absolutism. Likewise, without an appreciation of the notion of universality functioning as a check on the economy of difference, we cannot avoid epistemological and ethical relativism.

As we shall see, the "Discours préliminaire" provides readers with the tools to question both universalist and particularist claims about knowledge by engaging them in a productive mutual critique. For d'Alembert, the universalist belief that human beings can produce true knowledge that is subject to verification and agreement does not necessarily contradict the assumption that such knowledge is mediated and relative. The "Discours" grants that knowledge depends upon and may change according to human cognitive tools, biases, and cultural contexts.

CHAPTER THREE

At the same time, the text also suggests that knowledge, when acquired through the right methods, yields an accurate anthropocentric perception of the world. By navigating a course between relativism and universalism, the "Discours préliminaire" encourages the human quest for accurate descriptions of the world while at the same time allowing for open-ended debates about their accuracy and value.

The *Encyclopédie* in the Context of Contemporary Scholarly Debates

Why do I regard d'Alembert's "Discours préliminaire" as an optimal point of departure for changing the way we interpret Enlightenment epistemology? First, because I consider this text to be representative of the richness of Enlightenment debates about the nature of truth. The "Discours" introduces the objectives of one of the most important Enlightenment projects, the *Encyclopédie*. No doubt, as numerous critics point out, the highly diversified articles of the *Encyclopédie* cannot be reduced to d'Alembert's view of the project.[9] Nonetheless, the "Discours" functions as a prospectus that indicates what many of the Enlighteners proposed to do in their joint enterprise. Second, as Daniel Brewer has shown, d'Alembert's introduction elaborates the distinctly modern[10] and nuanced understanding of knowledge and value that emerged during the French Enlightenment. This legacy cannot be described solely in terms of universalist thought. Undoubtedly, the tendency toward universalization plays an important role in Enlightenment philosophy. Along with a process of exclusion of the particular to create the false unity of universal concepts, however, we also encounter in the *Encyclopédie* self-critical elements that undermine universalist paradigms.

Scholars generally agree that the French Enlightenment cannot be reduced to a universalist logic. Most critics, however, tend to juxtapose the epistemological openness of some Enlightenment philosophes with the dogmatism of others. According to contemporary criticism, Diderot's work serves as a model of an open-ended epistemology.[11] Conversely, d'Alembert's writing is described as trapped in a closed universalist framework that is not far removed from Cartesian rationalism.[12] In response to such scholarship, I will identify the openness and internal contradictions of d'Alembert's epistemology. Before I explain how my argument differs from and expands upon previous scholarship on the subject, let me describe briefly some of the arguments that resemble my own.

Several scholars have emphasized the self-consciously contradictory elements of Enlightenment epistemology. In *Diderot: Le Labyrinthe de la Relation*, for example, Pierre Saint-Amand analyzes the tension between the *Encyclopédie*'s attempt to establish indubitable foundations for human knowledge and its skepticism toward all foundational thought. He argues that the metaphors of the labyrinth (*le labyrinthe*) and the world map (*la mappemonde*) capture this tension. The labyrinth functions as an analogue for the disorder and ultimate incomprehensibility of nature. By way of contrast, the world map symbolizes the human effort to master both the unruliness of nature and the multiplicity and contradictions of human perception. The labyrinth therefore sketches a relativist epistemology riddled by the confusion of the universe and the incommensurable variety of human representations. Conversely, the world map outlines a universalist epistemology that purports to offer accurate descriptions of the world. The term "complexity," Saint-Amand demonstrates, captures the *Encyclopédie*'s attempt to reconcile order and disorder, certainty and doubt:

> *Complexity* means simultaneously order and disorder, process. The term also retains its closely related sense of complication, in order to say that in a system there is quantifiable information, large groups, randomness, a code which escapes us. Finally, complexity represents not so much a term as a structure: order-disorder-paradox. [13]

Saint-Amand's reading of the *Encyclopédie* in terms of its philosophical complexity suggests that the tension between order and disorder we encounter in its articles exceeds the logic of mere contradiction. On one level, this tension organizes the entire (static) structure of the text, which juxtaposes the partial and often contradictory information provided by the individual articles with the overarching attempt to provide the truth of nature and society as a whole. On another level, the tension between order and disorder, fragment and whole, motivates a (dynamic) intellectual process that incites generations of readers to question the various truth-claims proposed by the *Encyclopédie*.

Christie V. McDonald's *Dialogue of Writing: Essays in Eighteenth-Century French Literature*[14] and James Creech's *Diderot: Thresholds of Representation*[15] further explore the implications of the *Encyclopédie*'s tendency to present knowlege both as representation—and therefore subject to human bias and distortion—and as unmediated truth itself. According to Creech, "The 'Discours préliminaire' expresses the well-known Enlightenment program that for d'Alembert no less than for us was the 'true nature' of the Encyclopedic project. But it also writes large the impossibility of these founding ideological a *prioris* that contribute its 'true nature' (its identity as Encyclopedia), thus undermining itself to a remarkable degree" (10). If the *Encyclopédie* undermines its own truth-claims by arguing that all knowledge, even the most scientific, is ultimately a form of representation, does it therefore lapse into epistemological relativism? In other words, we are led to ask, to what extent does the *Encyclopédie* undo its main goal of providing a better kind of knowledge than pre-Enlightenment texts?

This is precisely the question posed by Daniel Brewer's *The Discourse of Enlightenment*. Brewer asks:

> If the eighteenth-century Enlighteners sought their freedom by refusing the paradigms and principles that unshakably grounded knowledge in religious and metaphysical terms, do they undo in the process the foundation of knowledge in general, including that of their own epistemological systems? If they reject the universals that underpinned the ethics, esthetics, and social theory of a prior age, what of the ultimate ground of their own theoretical enterprises in such domains?[16]

Brewer answers his own question by arguing that, for the Enlighteners, questioning the objective foundations of knowledge did not conflict with their project of providing more valuable forms of knowledge. In other words, Brewer argues, the Enlighteners wished to have it both ways. They combined a skeptical attitude toward the process of acquiring knowledge with an objectivist quest for truth:

> If the problem of defining the Enlightenment critically marks the limits of modern philosophy, it is because philosophy can be modern only by becoming caught in what could be called the double bind of Enlightenment.... The knots of this double bind begin to tighten as the eighteenth-century Enlighteners endeavor to free themselves from the fetters of what they call ignorance, superstition, and religious dogma. They attempt to produce knowledge at its most useful, insisting above all on the arbitrary status of any way of representing knowledge.[17]

I would like to explore further the implications of this seemingly contradictory Enlightenment epistemology, which other scholars have described in terms of its complexity, the symbolic tension between metaphor and metonymy, and the double bind between unmediated truth and distorted representation. As noted, I argue that the seemingly paradoxical epistemology of the "Discours préliminaire" can be explained in terms of a dialectical process that combines aspects of universalism and particularism while ultimately rejecting both. In so doing, the "Discours préliminaire" goes beyond the poor alternative of either forsaking the possibility of true knowledge or accepting closed definitions of truth.

Displacing Philosophical Precursors: Empiricist versus/and Rationalist Epistemology

For both critics and enthusiasts of Enlightenment thought, the *Encyclopédie* offers a logical starting point for an investigation of how representations of the subject intersect with distinctly modern means of producing knowledge. No other body of texts provides greater insight into the systems of classification produced during the Enlightenment in France than the *Encyclopédie*. Initially, the *Encyclopédie, ou Dictionnaire Raisonné des Sciences, des Arts et des Métiers* (1745–72) was conceived by its editors, Denis Diderot and Jean Le Rond d'Alembert, as an imitation of Ephraim Chambers's two-volume *Cyclopaedia* (1728). Although its editors envisioned a small work, the *Encyclopédie* turned out to be a vast and revolutionary project.[18] Rather than faithfully recording acquired knowledge, it generated an epistemological system that provided a new understanding of human moral and political identity. The *Encyclopédie* did not, however, completely reject previous intellectual history. As Michel Foucault illustrates in *The Order of Things*, the *Encyclopédie* built upon and helped undermine Cartesian rationalism.[19] D'Alembert introduces the *Encyclopédie* by tracing the intellectual history of this project. Appropriately, he spends a great deal of time acknowledging Descartes's influence as well as the *Encyclopédie*'s departure from rationalism. "Descartes", he explains,

> was undoubtedly wrong in accepting the notion of innate ideas. Had he retained from the peripatetic sect the only truth it taught concerning the

CHAPTER THREE

origination of ideas from the senses, perhaps the errors, which blended with and undermined this truth, would have been harder to uproot. At least Descartes dared to teach the learned to escape the yoke of scholasticism, opinion and authority: in other words the prejudices of barbarism.... If he ended up believing that he explained everything, at least he began by doubting everything. The arms we employ to attack him belong to him even if we turn them against him. (xxv-xxvi)

Certainly, d'Alembert observes, the Cartesian method, given its reliance upon the notions of innate ideas and theologically guaranteed truths, may not have provided the right foundations for his own rationalist-materialist theory of knowledge. Nonetheless, he qualifies, the Enlighteners could build upon elements of the Cartesian tradition. By engaging in a methodical doubt that questioned former (Scholasticist) methods of acquiring knowledge and, furthermore, by insisting upon modes of demonstration based upon phenomenological experiences, the Cartesian method provided the eighteenth-century sensationalists, materialists, and empiricists with the means of simultaneously validating and questioning their own methods and assumptions.[20]

Although I will not offer a detailed analysis of Descartes's *Discours de la Méthode* (1637), I would like to encapsulate briefly some of the features that proved indispensable to d'Alembert's self-critical, and often anti-universalist, epistemology. As we recall, Descartes attempted to find truth-certainty about our perception of ourselves and of the world. He hoped to eliminate all sources of error by placing under methodical doubt both the accuracy of perception and the assumptions of Scholastic philosophy. We could say that Descartes's methodical doubt observed a double dialectical process, moving first from false universals to relativism, then from relativism back to a truer form of universal knowledge.

True knowledge, observes Descartes, can only be attained by rejecting (or negating) the universals associated with both commonplace knowledge and Scholastic epistemology. This process of elimination of false certainties leads Descartes to doubt everything except, of course, his own ability to doubt.[21] After having discarded such universals, Descartes is left without a strong foundation for knowledge. He lapses momentarily into the epistemological relativism of the subjective self (or *cogito*), whose only claim to truth remains the ability to think. Describing human beings in terms of this minimal function does not, however, satisfy Descartes's quest for truth-certainty.

To attain objective knowledge of the universe, the philosopher proceeds to endow the subjective self with some generalizable qualities and criteria of validation. He groups these qualities and criteria together under the notion of "clear and distinct ideas." Consequently, after having rejected universalism by interjecting a relativist perspective, Descartes dispels radical doubt by moving from the particular back to the universal. Universal standards, or what he calls "moral maxims," are formed by means of the negation of the relativism associated with the plurality of views and the unreliability of human perception that he had postulated earlier. It would seem as if Descartes were contradicting himself. He is not, however, because the universalism he rejects is not the same as the one he proposes. As we recall, Descartes used relativism to reject false universals. He then proceeds to imagine a better form of universalism to displace his momentary (and disingenuous) relativism. As an architect of rationalist epistemology, Descartes rebuilds the foundation of truth by positing the validity of "the laws and the customs of his country," and, above all, by "firmly holding on" to faith in God. For Descartes, the divine functions as the ultimate universal guarantee of the validity of human knowledge.

God becomes the standard of universal truth by being defined as the contrary of the relativistic *cogito*. According to Descartes's dialectical model, the divine lacks (or negates) all the imperfection, particularities, and contingencies that characterize the human.[22] The philosopher thus employs the figure of God to revalidate, one by one, the certainties he has placed under methodical doubt, including the existence of the self, the external world, and true knowledge. If we adopt a dialectical logic, it follows that if man is imperfect, then God is perfect; if man is finite, then God is infinite; and if man has partial knowledge, then God, his creator, must have complete knowledge. Insofar as human beings are created by a perfect and all-powerful divinity, Descartes deduces, it cannot be that all of our faculties are deceptive. Such reasoning leads the philosopher to his (in)famous conception of humans as beings whose souls share God's perfection but whose bodies or senses are imperfect and unreliable. This dualist ontology reflects the two sides of the double dialectical process Descartes followed to dismantle prejudice and rebuild truth. The first dialectical movement, established through a process of methodical doubt that negates older models of validity, leads Descartes to describe human sensory perception as relative and hence unreliable. Conversely, the second dialectical movement, established through a process of universalization that negates

CHAPTER THREE

former sources of doubt, leads him to depict the soul as the faculty that generates "clear and distinct" and hence accurate perceptions of the world.

In the next step of his proof, Descartes mobilizes the idea of God to describe human beings as composed of both fallible body (the source of unreliable, relative knowledge) and infallible soul (the font of universal truth).[23] The philosopher then proceeds to outline a rational process that compensates for the fallibility of sense perception. Nonetheless, as Descartes's many critics indicate, the two sides of human nature are never fully reconciled. Descartes provides no satisfactory explanation of how soul and body communicate so well that, rather than the soul interpreting the unreliable sensations perceived by the body, misleading sensory perceptions are corrected by the soul. The double dialectical movements between universalist and particularist claims pursued by Cartesian philosophy consequently do not produce a stable synthesis between doubt and knowledge. Instead, they yield a sublation, or partial incorporation and negation, of both relativism and universalism. Cartesian philosophy thus embodies the beginnings of a double dialectical process. On the one hand, such a theory uses particularist claims to question universalist certainties. On the other hand, it also uses universalism as a regulatory ideal that dispels relativist doubts. This is precisely the double movement developed further by d'Alembert.

D'Alembert's Epistemology: Beyond the Particular and the Universal

D'Alembert avows that he is particularly drawn to the self-critical aspects of Cartesian philosophy. He notes approvingly, "If he [Descartes] ended up believing that he explained everything, at least he began by doubting everything" (xxvi). D'Alembert's statement suggests that Descartes can be regarded as the founder of a form of critical reasoning that inaugurates the beginnings of modernity. So far I have noted that, in claiming that empiricism relies upon preceding rationalist methods of producing knowledge, d'Alembert acknowledges the "genealogical" filiation between rationalism and materialism. Let me now elaborate what d'Alembert means by such a genealogy and how it relates to the problem of universalist versus particularist epistemologies. To explain the interpenetration of rationalist and materialist methods, d'Alembert proposes a definition of genealogy that identifies both epistemological ruptures and affinities among different fields of study:

> The first step that we have to take in this research is to examine the genealogy, so to speak, and the filiation of our knowledge, the causes which produced it and its distinguishing characteristics: in a word, to arrive at the origin and generation of our ideas. (i)

Like Descartes, d'Alembert maps out the domain of knowledge by negotiating between particularist and universalist assumptions. Genealogical classification, proceeds d'Alembert, if it is to be both comprehensive and sufficiently detailed, must follow a hermeneutic process that constantly mediates between the universal and the particular:

> The work whose first volume we are presenting today has two objectives: as an *Encyclopedia* it should illuminate, as much as possible, the order and connections of human knowledge; as a Dictionary, it should identify the general principles which establish each Science and each Art as well as identify the most essential details of each branch of knowledge. (i)

On the one hand, as an encyclopedia, the *Encyclopédie* must ascertain the order and connections among different domains of human knowledge. The text attains such a level of comprehensiveness and generality only when it excludes, by observing a dialectical process, the particular features of each field.

On the other hand, d'Alembert continues, as a dictionary, the *Encyclopédie* must also focus upon the individual features of each field. The text delves into details only when it excludes, following an opposing dialectical movement, the intersections and connections among different disciplines. Establishing a double dialectical relation between the particular and the general, the *Encyclopédie* thus presents a system of knowledge that provides more information than does the sum of its parts. Because the text juxtaposes and compares the arts and sciences, d'Alembert can assert that the different disciplines "aid each other, and consequently a common thread ties them together" (i). He qualifies, however, that maintaining an equilibrium between the particular and the general remains a difficult task: "If it is often difficult to reduce each Science or Art to a small set of rules or general principles, it is equally difficult to contain within one system the infinitely diverse branches of human science" (i). Given

CHAPTER THREE

that d'Alembert acknowledges the difficulty of systematizing information, we are led to ask: What unifies the "infinitely varied" articles of the *Encyclopédie* into a coherent and systematic tree of knowledge? Or, to paraphrase Christie McDonald, what is the epistemological relation between the fragment (the particular) and the whole (the universal) established by the "Discours"?

D'Alembert answers this question by explaining, "The encyclopedic order does not suppose that all the sciences relate directly to one another. They are branches of the same trunk of human knowledge. Often these branches do not have an immediate connection, and many of them are connected only by the trunk itself" (xix). What unifies knowledge therefore is not so much the inherent links among different fields as human cognition itself. Knowledge, d'Alembert observes, is necessarily anthropocentric. Human beings produce and classify their descriptions of the world, thus transforming the contingency and disorder of nature into a seemingly organic tree of knowledge. By describing knowledge in terms of the arbitrary systems of classification that organize the *Encyclopédie*, however, d'Alembert could, indeed, be interpreted as arguing that human knowledge is relative.[24] As carefully as he avoided universalist epistemology, however, the philosopher sidesteps relativism by adding:

> [The encyclopedic order] consists of gathering information in the smallest possible space and in placing, so to speak, the philosopher above this vast labyrinth in an elevated spot from which he can perceive simultaneously the main arts and sciences; ascertain at a glance the objects of his speculations and the operations that he can perform upon these objects; distinguish the branches of human knowledge, the points which unite or separate them; and even distinguish the secret paths which bring them together. (xv)

Having exposed the arbitrary nature of knowledge by showing its dependency upon competing systems of classification, d'Alembert proceeds to reclaim its universalist foundations.

Although knowledge may not be objective, he maintains, neither is it relative. Human beings should be able to distinguish between valid and invalid methods of producing information. The best system of classification, d'Alembert suggests, is one that eliminates the disorder of the world and of human perception. Once we pursue a dialectical process that eliminates all particularities and contingencies from the production of knowledge, we are left with a singular and seemingly universal perspective.

D'Alembert compares this perspective to a philosophical bird's-eye view of the world. The universal knower imagined by d'Alembert, however, does not provide an objective description of the world. Such a subject presents instead the most comprehensive and elegant representation of the world: meaning, as Brewer has illustrated, one that is best grasped by and most useful to human beings.[25] To explain the seemingly contradictory proposition that knowledge can be both true and nonobjective, d'Alembert draws one of the most well-known analogies of the "Discours":

> It is a kind of world map that shows the main countries, their position and their interdependency, the straight path that connects them—a path which is often cut by a thousand obstacles that are known in each country only to its inhabitants or to travelers, and that would be shown only in very detailed maps. These specific maps will be the different articles of the *Encyclopédie*, and the tree or represented system will be the world map. (xv)

By employing the metaphor of a totalizing *mappemonde* to correlate the articles of the *Encyclopédie*, d'Alembert appears to observe a dialectical process that displaces one form of epistemological universalism (objectivism) with another (anthropocentric universalism). As we recall, objectivism asserts that human descriptions of the world capture the way the world is. More modestly, anthropocentric universalism claims that, although humans may not be able to perceive the universe accurately, there is only one valid human perspective of it. D'Alembert quite literally embodies this perspective in the figure of "the philosopher [placed] above this vast labyrinth in an elevated spot from which he can perceive simultaneously the main arts and sciences" (xv).

This philosophical bird's-eye view, d'Alembert explains, is universal because it is shared (potentially) by all human beings. The philosopher epitomizes the privileged universal subject not because he has superior innate faculties, but because, unlike most human beings, he devotes his intellectual abilities to the pursuit of knowledge. At the same time, d'Alembert's epistemology implies that, insofar as other human beings do not share the opinions of the (imaginary) universal subject, their knowledge can only be partial, incomplete, and erroneous. Difference thus becomes reincorporated into sameness. If all humans, indeed, if whatever is essentialized as human nature itself, share cognitive abilities that enable them to have the same knowledge of the world, then this knowledge cannot be considered relative. On the contrary, at least from a human perspective, anthropocentric knowledge can be accepted as not only reliable, but also as universally valid. Let us now examine how d'Alembert first establishes, and then proceeds to undermine, the universality of human cognition. To do so, we must return to an earlier part of the "Discours," where the philosopher elaborates a definition of being that complements his theory of knowledge.

After describing the *Encyclopédie*'s genealogical method, d'Alembert portrays the human subject capable of producing such knowledge.

> Our knowledge can be categorized as either direct or dependent upon thought. Direct knowledge is that which we obtain immediately, without any act of volition. . . . Knowledge that depends upon thought is acquired by uniting and combining direct knowledge. (i–ii)

Like Descartes, d'Alembert describes the materialist subject in terms of his physical and mental capacities. Rather than conceptualizing the "homo duplex" ontologically as a split between perfect soul and imperfect body, however, d'Alembert divides man epistemologically in terms of two complementary modes of acquiring knowledge. By means of direct and immediate sensations, we, human beings, perceive ourselves and the external world. In turn, our rational or "reflective" faculties select, combine, and interpret sensory data. To guarantee the validity of those interpretations, however, d'Alembert must first establish that the sensations which are organized by our rational faculties are reliable themselves.

The materialist philosopher plans to avoid the epistemological trouble encountered by Cartesian rationalism by assuming, rather than attempting to prove, the reliability of sense perceptions: "Nothing is more incontestable," d'Alembert maintains, "than the existence of our sensations; thus to prove that they are the principle of all our knowledge, it suffices to prove that they can be: because, according to philosophy, deductions that are based upon facts or recognized truths are preferable to those that are based upon hypotheses, even ingenious ones" (ii). This statement, however, remains ambiguous. It is not altogether clear: What is incontestable according to d'Alembert—the fact that we have sensations or the fact that our sensations accurately depict the world we perceive? D'Alembert's assertion that, in order to show that sensations serve as the reliable foundation for knowledge, it suffices to prove that they *could* serve as such, does not solve his problem. Logically, showing that a phenomenon is possible does not prove that it occurs. Readers are thus confronted with two options. They can either regard d'Alembert's proof as unsatisfactory, or they can accept his founding of knowledge upon sense perceptions as axiomatic. By openly acknowledging his philosophical weakness—namely, that the validity of his assertions cannot be demonstrated—d'Alembert creates a paradoxical epistemology that contains the germ of its own critique. Starting with this rather unfoundational foundation, the philosopher continues to detail what humans can learn from their sensory experience.

Like Descartes, d'Alembert maintains that our first awareness is of our existence. "The first thing that our sensations teach us, a thing that is not separate from them, is our existence; from this it follows that our first reflections must refer to ourselves, that is to say, to the thinking principle that constitutes our nature and is not different from us" (ii). He elaborates, "The second knowledge that we owe to our sensations is the existence of external objects, among which belongs our body, because it is, so to speak, exterior to us even before we have distinguished the nature of the reflective principle within us" (ii). Another question presents itself in light of d'Alembert's account of the interaction between body and mind. If, like Descartes, he describes the body as external to the "reflective principle within us," then how do mind and body interact to provide reliable sensory impressions? Is there any relation, or, more strictly, a correspondence, between the way we perceive the material world and the way the world is?

Once again, d'Alembert interjects doubt rather than certainty into his apparently universalist theory of knowledge. He insists that there is no demonstrable correlation between our sensations and the objects we perceive: "Indeed, since there is no connection among sensations and the object which causes them, or at least in which we relate to them, it seems that we cannot find the linking principle that connects them. Only a kind of instinct, more certain than reason itself, can make us overcome such a great gap" (ii). As before, he asks readers to assume the correspondence between perception and objects of perception as axiomatic. Adopting a conversational tone, he assures readers that even the most skeptical philosophers no longer question this correlation. His goal is neither to question "a truth which is recognized and undisputed by the skeptics," nor to proclaim the objectivity of human knowledge, a problem that he leaves up to the "enlightened Metaphysicians to develop its principle" (ii). Time and

CHAPTER THREE

again, the "Discours préliminaire" undermines the possibility of certain knowledge of the world. It does so by negating the correspondence between world and perception (which, d'Alembert maintains, cannot be empirically shown or logically proven) while simultaneously asserting the credibility of such a belief (humans should act as if it were true).

Having undermined objectivism, d'Alembert proceeds to undermine the anthropocentric form of universalist epistemology as well:

> Just as in the general maps of the world that we inhabit, objects are more or less close to one another and present a different sight depending upon the point of view of the geographer who constructed the map, so the form of the encyclopedic tree depends upon the perspective from which we consider the literary universe. We can thus imagine as many different systems of human knowledge as there are worldmaps; and each of these systems might have some advantages that others lack. (xv)

By excluding all universal standards from the production of knowledge, d'Alembert moves even closer to epistemological relativism. Human knowledge, he claims, is not unitary after all. What seems to be a good description of the world from one perspective is a poor description from another. Ultimately, humans cannot agree upon the philosophical bird's-eye view postulated earlier. Systems of classification themselves are dependent upon the points of view of those who have produced them. Consequently, d'Alembert argues, adopting classically relativist terminology, we can imagine as many systems of classification as there are ways of seeing the world from various locations. Each perspective has certain advantages that the others lack. Does it follow that all "world maps," or all methods of acquiring knowledge, are equally (in)valid?

No, it does not, d'Alembert asserts, once again introducing universalist standards into his momentarily relativist theory of knowledge. To offset relativism, he proposes some criteria of distinguishing good from bad systems of classification of information. At the same time, he stands by his former claim that even the best forms of knowledge cannot provide unmediated access to the truth:

> Whatever the case may be, the tree of knowledge that offers the most links and connections among the sciences is preferable, without a doubt, to all others. Yet we can flatter ourselves of capturing it? . . . The universe is nothing but a vast ocean, whose surface is covered with a few islands of different sizes, whose connections to the continent remains unknown. (xv)

The epistemology d'Alembert presents through a series of dialectical moves from (objectivist and anthropocentric) universalism to relativism plausibly intertwines faith and doubt in the validity of knowledge. The philosopher reiterates that the encyclopedia which can offer the most elegant connections among the various disciplines it presents is, indeed, preferable to the others. Nonetheless, the information conveyed by that encyclopedia can be improved upon by future generations. By acknowledging that, like all human creations, the *Encyclopédie* is subject to error, d'Alembert expresses the Enlighteners' sense of intellectual modesty and openness to competing visions of the world. At the same time, the "Discours" suggests that without criteria of validity—that is, without some more or less shared yet negotiable standards—debates about the nature of truth or reality become meaningless. In combining a genuine quest for universal truth with the relativist acknowledgment that such a truth may never be reached or, at least, that there may be several paths that can lead to it, the *Encyclopédie* offers a useful alternative to the dilemma of choosing between relativism and universalism. This open attitude toward knowledge has implications for both ontology and ethics. If truth claims must be argued for and can be contested, then definitions of humanity as well as the boundaries between ethical and unethical behavior are also subject to discussion.

In my analysis of the "Discours préliminaire," I began to sketch such an alternative cultural logic that selectively combines, rather than displaces, universalist and particularist standards. By arguing for the necessity of developing a double dialectical relation between particularist and universalist epistemological claims, I have attempted to offer a possible answer to Naomi Schor's timely question: "what becomes of universality in an era of ever more marginal subjectivities, ever more anti-universalist gender disorders? According to what logic can particularism flourish, severed from the universal? Or to put it more bluntly: is the universal worth saving? Or, more cautiously: is there anything in the classic conception of the universal that is worth saving?"[26] My essay maintained that both particular and universal standards are worth saving and, moreover, that the two should be regarded as not only conceptually but also normatively inseparable. Along with critics such as Richard Bernstein[27] and Naomi Schor,[28] I argue that the goal is not to eliminate the universal, but "to arrive at a new universal that would include all those who wish to be included and that would above all afford them the opportunity to speak universal while not relinquishing their difference(s)."[29] Although I do not claim (or even wish) to prescribe the content of this new universality, I have suggested that one way in which it can be produced is by establishing a double dialectical relation between particularist and universalist standards. In a double dialectical process, the category of difference serves to ward off epistemological and ethical absolutism. Analogously, the category of universality serves as a flexible standard used to negotiate the possibilities of human knowledge. The critical and, indeed, necessary tension between universalist and relativist standards that we encounter in Enlightenment texts has produced a complex philosophical system that could be regarded as a fruitful beginning for the elaboration of an epistemology, ontology, and ethics of our postmodern world.

Notes

1. This essay appeared in *Eighteenth-Century Studies*, vol. 33, no. 3 (2000), 383–400 and in *Perusals into Postmodern Thought*, 2000.

2. I am using the term "dialectic" in a Hegelian sense, to indicate a conceptual and historical process of achieving progress by means of a series of sublations (or the selective negation of undesirable qualities and incorporation of desirable qualities into a later stage of development). I describe d'Alembert's thought as "dialectical" because I believe that Hegel systematized most elegantly a process that was already employed by previous philosophers, including d'Alembert.

3. All references to the "Discours préliminaire" are to the facsimile of the first edition published between 1751 and 1780 of the *Encyclopédie ou Dictionnaire Raisonné des Sciences, des Arts et des Métiers*. All translations from the "Discours" are my own.

4. See Jürgen Habermas's *The Theory of Communicative Action*.

5. Because relativism maintains that there are multiple particular versions of the truth, I will use the terms relativism and particularism interchangeably.

6. See Michel Foucault's *The Order of Things*.

7. Bernstein, *Beyond Objectivism and Relativism: Science, Hermeneutics and Praxis*, 3.

8. I am borrowing the term "double dialectics" from Luce Irigaray's *An Ethics of Sexual Difference*. In this work, Irigaray uses the terms "chiasmus" or the "double dialectics" as a metaphor for a yet unachieved sexual reciprocity and equivalence between women and men. For an exposition of Irigaray's use of the metaphor of a "chiasmus" or "double dialectic" to critique Hegelian thought, see my book, *Gender and Citizenship: A Genealogy of Subject-Citizenship in Nineteenth-Century French Literature and Culture*. I employ the term "double dialectics" not as a metaphor, however, but as an explanation of a semiotic process that overcomes binary hierarchies, including the one established between the relative and the universal.

9. In *Diderot's Dream*, for example, Wilda Anderson juxtaposes Diderot's and d'Alembert's visions of the *Encyclopédie*. She states: "Diderot's meditations, in the famous article 'Encyclopédie,' demonstrate this split. This article constitutes a quite striking example of what will come to be the characteristic Diderotian writing stance resulting from his notion of all activity as interaction, for it is a direct response to d'Alembert's 'Discours préliminaire'" (5). By way of contrast, my reading underscores the nondogmatic nature of d'Alembert's "Discours."

10. See Daniel Brewer's *The Discourse of Enlightenment in Eighteenth-Century France: Diderot and the Art of Philosophizing*.

11. For example, in *Diderot: Le Labyrinthe de la Relation*, Pierre Saint-Amand argues that Diderot employs the image of the map in a more complex and less linear fashion than d'Alembert.

12. Wilda Anderson persuasively demonstrates the continuity between Cartesian rationalism and d'Alembert's materialist rationalism in *Diderot's Dream*.

13. Saint-Amand, 16 (my translation).

14. In *Dialogue of Writing: Essays in Eighteenth-Century French Literature*, Christie V. McDonald describes the double nature of the *Encyclopédie*—vacillating between fragmentary articles that disperse knowledge and its totalizing project of capturing all knowledge—in terms of the symbolic shifts between metonymy (or the part) and metaphor (or the whole): "Finally, the 'work of the text' is to elaborate a system in which the fragment leads to the whole, in which the dialogue between the articles attests once again to language as communication within a staunchly monologic—or utopian—system. In contrast, the 'text of the work' is that which disrupts the system, isolates the fragment, disperses dialogue into the endless interference of reading with writing, and makes possible only local—not universal—meaning" (88).

15. See James Creech's *Diderot: Thresholds of Representation*.

16. Brewer, 5.

17. Brewer, 2.

18. As Daniel Brewer documents in *The Discourse of Enlightenment*, by 1772 the *Encyclopédie* comprised seventeen volumes containing 71,818 articles and eleven volumes containing 2,885 plates.

19. In *The Order of Things*, Michel Foucault argues that Descartes and d'Alembert, or more generally, rationalism and empiricism, share epistemic foundations. He contends, "One has the impression—and it is often expressed—that the history of nature must have appeared as Cartesian mechanism ebbed. . . . Unfortunately, things do not happen as simply as that. It is quite possible . . . that one science can arise out of another; but no science can be generated by the absence of another . . . mechanism from Descartes to d'Alembert and natural history from Tournefort to Daubenton were authorized by the same episteme" (128).

20. As John C. O'Neal notes in *The Authority of Experience: Sensationist Theory in the French Enlightenment*, the concepts of empiricism, sensationism, and material-

ism overlap, and thus are often used interchangeably. All three theories proposed that knowledge is derived from observation of the phenomenal world. To begin distinguishing these concepts, we might say that empiricism refers to an epistemology which posits that knowledge is derived from experience; materialism refers to an ontology which assumes that the real world is made up of matter (as opposed to ideas); while sensationism, as O'Neal indicates, refers to a more focused intellectual movement during the Enlightenment which argued for the sensory origin of ideas (smell, touch, sight, hearing). Generally speaking, d'Alembert's epistemology can be called empiricist because it takes into account the knowledge provided by observation. Most often, however, I refer to d'Alembert's epistemology more specifically as "materialist rationalist" because it combines the belief that the universe is physical or material with the assumption that the universe can be known through a combination of abstract reasoning and observation.

21. Descartes states: "But having learned since my school days that one cannot imagine anything so strange or unbelievable that it has not been said by some philosopher, and, since then, during my travels, having acknowledged that those who have feelings quite contrary to our own are not for that reason barbarians or savages, . . . I could find no one whose opinions, it seemed to me, ought to be preferred over the others, and I found myself constrained to try to lead myself on my own" (8–9). In the footnotes, I will be citing from *Discourse on Method*, translated by Donald A. Cress.

22. Descartes continues, "For, following from the reasonings I have just given, to know the nature of God, as far as my own nature was able, I had only to consider each thing about which I found an idea in myself, whether or not it was a perfection to have them, and I was certain that none of those that were marked by any imperfection were in this nature, but that all other perfections were. So I observed that doubt, inconstancy, sadness and the like could not be in him, given the fact that I would have been happy to be exempt from them. Now, over and above that, I had ideas of several sensible and corporeal things; for even supposing that I was dreaming and that everything I saw or imagined was false, I still could not deny that the ideas were not truly in my thought" (19).

23. Descartes deduces, "since I had already recognized very clearly in my case that intelligent nature is distinct from corporeal nature, taking into consideration that all composition attests to dependence and that dependence is manifestly a defect, I therefore judged that being composed of these two natures cannot be a perfection in God and that, as a consequence, God is not composed" (19).

24. The arbitrary aspects of the *Encyclopédie* I am referring to include its alphabetical order, the differing opinions expressed by the text, and its selection of certain qualities and functions of objects as opposed to others.

25. As Brewer observes in *The Discourse of Enlightenment*, "The order of things in the *Encyclopédie* is determined above all by the status accorded them as belongings, by their usefulness to an ordering subject. Things in the encyclopedic text do

not simply exist, they are meant to be used, and the products of their use are their value, which is one reason for the countless images of tools and machines in the encyclopedic plates" (19).

26. Schor, *Bad Objects: Essays Popular and Unpopular*, 16.

27. See, for example, Bernstein's attempt to move philosophical debates beyond the impasse of relativist and universalist ethics in *The New Constellation: The Ethical-Political Horizons of Modernity/Postmodernity*.

28. I am referring in particular to Naomi Schor's call for a reevaluation of the value of some open universalist norms in her essay "French Feminism is a Universalism," found in *Bad Objects*.

29. Schor, 26.

CHAPTER FOUR

An Ethics of Cultural Exchange: Diderot's *Supplément au Voyage de Bougainville*

Are there any universal—or singular, eternal, and static—moral standards that all human societies and groups should adopt regardless of cultural differences? In other words, is *universalist ethics* a desirable or even possible moral option in a multicultural world? Contemporary critics of universalism argue that such ethics turn out to be a form of cultural chauvinism, a way of imposing culturally specific standards upon societies where they would not be useful or appropriate. Even the most seemingly universalist rules—such as the injunctions not to harm or steal from other people—are always created by particular cultures or groups to serve their interests. Such injunctions, the argument goes, involve culturally specific and recent rather than atemporal and cross-cultural principles.[1] They depend upon the notion of the sanctity of the individual, human life, and property which, at least in Europe, emerged during the eighteenth century with the decline of aristocratic regimes and rise of an increasingly powerful middle class.

If we accept the proposition that universalism is, indeed, always a form of ethnocentrism that is blind to its own biases, then are we led to the conclusion that cultural relativism is the only plausible ethical theory modern societies can adopt? Should cultural differences preclude all societies or groups from judging one another? Without universal values, however, the very notion of ethics risks meaninglessness. This kind of reasoning oscillates between the poles of universalism and relativism without settling on either. If neither universalism nor relativism can adequately solve ethical problems, however, then what kind of ethical theory can? Is a path between universalism and relativism possi-

75

ble? What form would it take? I believe that Diderot's *Supplément au Voyage de Bougainville* (1770)[2] represents one of the most significant attempts to come to terms with ethical differences among and within cultures undertaken by eighteenth-century French fiction.

Diderot's *Supplément* is a fictitious supplement to a French explorer's account of his visit to Tahiti. It consists of a series of conversations, anecdotes, and speeches by French explorers and Tahitians. The text contrasts not only two cultures—the French and the Tahitian—but also, and more importantly, two kinds of attitudes toward cultural exchange: an ethnocentric one that regards itself as universal and a more tolerant one that accepts some degree of cultural relativism. The only way to uphold the universality of one's own values, Diderot suggests paradoxically, is by respecting cultural differences, or the relative. Only this dual perspective affords a balance between relativism and universalism that ultimately critiques and rejects both extremes. To arrive at a moral equilibrium, the *Supplément* observes a doubled dialectical process. On the one hand, the narrative rejects (or negates) complete cultural relativism because it still upholds the superiority of one's own cultural ethics over those of others. On the other hand, the text also rejects (or negates) absolutist, and ultimately ethnocentric, universalism because it endorses respecting the values of a host society. Let us follow the doubled dialectical narrative process that leads to what might be called an ethics of cultural exchange; one, that is, which negates both relativism and universalism.

The *Supplément* begins by emphasizing cultural differences. Its series of monologues and dialogues contrast the happy and natural life of the Tahitians, and particularly their freer codes of sexual behavior, with the restrictive mores of French society. Consequently, ethical distinctions are translated into sexual differences. Gender-based behavior functions as a litmus test as to whether a society observes or violates the universal laws of nature. Diderot establishes a complex correlation between the laws of nature and the universalist ethics that should govern human behavior.[3] The emerging French Enlightenment discourse of natural laws and rights proposed by philosophes such as Rousseau, Montesquieu, and Diderot himself, a discourse that supposedly represents universal human values, becomes displaced upon Tahitian society. This displacement is openly acknowledged by the text.

Diderot indicates that readers will not have direct access to the words of the Tahitian people. The words of Orou, for example, the main Tahitian character, are subject to several translations by Spanish and then French explorers. As two of the French characters observe, Orou's ethical critiques and visions, are "modelé(s) à l'européene." (177) Like Montesquieu in the *Lettres persanes* (1721), Diderot fictionalizes other cultures in order to problematize the aspects of French aristocratic society that he considers dated and wants to change. It is therefore not surprising that Orou provides a typical Enlightenment critique of traditional Western values. Does this mean that Diderot's travel narrative has absolutely nothing to teach its readers about respect for other cultures? No, it does not. The *Supplément*, along with other travel narratives such as the *Lettres persanes* and *Lettres d'une Péruvienne* (1752), continue to interest contemporary scholars because they raise a question that is becoming increasingly pertinent today: how can one respect and fairly represent other cultures without pretending to abandon one's own cultural perspectives and values?[4] This question, more so than the critique of aristocratic French culture, is the main ethical problem explored by the *Supplément*.

In *Diderot: Thresholds of Representation*, for example, James Creech regards the irreconcilable ethical perspectives of the *Supplément* as an epistemological tension in modes of representation: "The conclusion I have been implying up to now is this: representation . . . brings with it a problem of similarity and difference. This problem fuels epistemological systems. It is what those systems are trying to accommodate, but the effort itself is incommodious" (19). To represent the polarity between what Creech calls the "centrifugal generality" of universalist claims about truth and the "centripetal historicity" of culturally specific perspectives, the *Supplément* takes the form of several nested dialogues. The dialogic form, as Dena Goodman explains in *Criticism in Action*,[5] not only allows for the expression of vastly different points of view, but also quite explicitly opens up the text to interpretation by readers. "Unlike drama," Goodman observes, "the dialogue's nonmimetic character calls for critical thought and distance on the part of readers. This distance, when looked at from another angle, defines the reader's position as firmly rooted in the real world, where political action can be taken" (142). This chapter will explain how the nested dialogues of the *Supplément* help create such a critical and potentially political public by encouraging readers to perceive the limitations of a hierarchical (or single dialectical) model of culture, while also making them aware of the advantages of a more open (or double dialectical) model of cultural exchange.[6]

The *Supplément* begins as a conversation between two typical French Enlightenment men, called simply "A" and "B." One of the Frenchmen has read Bougainville's account of his explorations of "exotic" parts of the world, including the island of Tahiti. "A" and "B" begin their discussion by establishing the credibility of the French explorer. Readers are informed that Bougainville was a mathematician: that is to say, well versed in the science that epitomized objectivity and universal knowledge during the Enlightenment. While mathematics may have truth-value, the two characters imply that it has very little use-value.[7] According to "A," the exploration of exotic lands, which yields both pleasure and useful information, could be described as the very opposite of an objective science. As speaker "A" sees it, Bougainville moves inexplicably from the objectivity and seriousness of math to the relativism and frivolity of exploration: "I don't understand anything about this man. The study of mathematics, which implies a sedentary life, filled his youthful years; and yet he passes suddenly from a meditative and retired lifestyle to the active, errant and dissipated occupation of explorer" (142).

The narrative does not leave readers, however, with this poor impression of Bougainville's credibility. Character "B" quickly points out that mathematics and travel provide complementary means of acquiring knowledge of the world and the universe: "If you suppose that a ship is nothing but a floating house and if you consider the navigator who crosses vast spaces, constrained and immobilized in a rather narrow space, you would see him going around the world on a plank just as you and I are going around the universe on our floor" (142). The map unites the seemingly incompatible fields of math and exploration by placing the former at the service of the latter. Consequently, character "B" concludes, travel narratives combine the best of both worlds: the seriousness, objectivity, and truth-value of mathematics with the practical information gathered by exploratory voyages.

After establishing the credibility of the text, "A" and "B" attempt to establish the trustworthiness of its author. Far from being an eccentric, one of the Frenchmen suggests, Bougainville is a reliable Enlightenment subject of knowledge who "left towards his pursuits with all the necessary insights and qualities: philosophy, courage, truth; a perspicacious glance that grasps things and shortens observation time; circumspection, patience; the desire to see and learn; the science of mathematics, mechanics, geometry and astronomy; and a sufficient smattering of natural history" (142). Such a well-rounded man is amply qualified to provide Europeans with information about the rest of the world, including the Philippines, New Holland, and unknown parts of Africa. Not only is

Bougainville instructive, but also, according to "B," he has a strong character. After all, we are reminded, Bougainville was courageous enough to have withstood battles with the sea, illness, fatigue, and hunger, among other perils.

The information gathered by Bougainville, however, is valuable less because it expands European knowledge of other cultures than because it teaches Europeans about themselves. Learning about supposedly primitive cultures allows Europeans to catch a glimpse of their own origins. As character "B" wonders, "Who knows the primitive history of our planet? How many places on earth which are now separate were once contiguous?" (143). "B" draws an analogy between geography and anthropology. Just as exploring the geographical features of non-European lands provides information about the origin of the Earth, so analyzing the behavior of their people provides information about the origin of advanced European civilizations.

Pursuing this line of thought, the two Frenchmen further speculate: what might have happened to the inhabitants of remote places who had to live in extremely small spaces? What kind of "cruel and necessary" practices did they follow to control the growth of their population? (144). Did they end up killing and eating each other to prevent starvation? Did they castrate their males? Did they infibulate their women? After envisioning the putative savagery of non-Western practices, the Frenchmen proceed to imagine the physiological monstrosity of the natives. According to some European travel narratives, one of the Frenchmen indicates, the Patagonians are "good people who come to you, and who kiss you as they shout *Chaoua*; they are strong, vigorous, while nonetheless not exceeding the height of five feet and five or six inches; not being large except in their corpulence, the size of their heads and the thickness of their members" (145).

The physical strength and deformity of the Patagonians is tempered, however, by the innocence of their behavior. The two Frenchmen regard native behavior as the origin of European politics. Just as the Europeans are aggressive to invaders and friendly to allies, so the savage "is sweet and innocent, as long as nothing disturbs his rest and security" (145). "B" proceeds to explain: "All war is born out of claims for the same property. Civilized man has a common claim with civilized man to the possession of a domain where they take opposite sides, and this domain becomes a subject of dispute between them" (145). European traditions thus are firmly founded upon supposedly natural, proprietary human instincts.

CHAPTER FOUR

Turning to Bougainville's story, character "B" summarizes the relation between European and non-European cultures:

> I don't doubt it: savage life is so simple, and our societies are such complicated machines! The Tahitian touches upon the origin of the world and the European upon its old age. The interval which separates him from us is greater than the distance between a new-born infant and an old man. He does not understand anything about our habits, our laws, in which he sees nothing but obstacles disguised in a hundred different ways; obstacles that can't but provoke the indignation and the disdain of a being in whom the sentiment of liberty is the strongest of sentiments. (146)

The discussion between the two Frenchmen reviews culturally entrenched assumptions about the nature of exploratory voyages: the belief that they constituted useful sources of information about human evolution and geographical change; that the explorer, if well-educated, was an objective (i.e., truthful and impartial) source of knowledge; and that Western cultures had attained the pinnacle of human civilization. As is generally the case in exotic narratives,[8] the two Frenchmen describe "savage life" with ambivalence rather than unqualified praise. "Savage life" lies far behind the stage of development and complexity of "civilized life." Character "B" uses the same analogy as La Mettrie—the man-machine—to contrast the simplicity of "primitive" societies with the complexity of "advanced" societies, "[that] are such complicated machines." From the analogy between man and machine, the text goes on to describe the relation between Europeans and natives in terms of two different—and distant—stages of human development: "The Tahitian touches upon the origin of the world and the European upon its old age."

Character "B" qualifies that this description of non-Western and Western man as part of the same evolutionary chain of development can only be analogical since "The interval which separates him from us is greater than the distance between a new-born infant and an old man." Using the language of natural history, character "B" compares non-European people to children and observes their practices in order to comprehend the more baffling behavior of "civilized man."[9] The relationship between the Western observers and the non-Western observed is obviously hierarchical and nonreciprocal, the product of a single dialectical understanding of cultural difference. For while Bougainville is assumed to have the expertise and authority to observe Tahitian behavior, the Tahitian subject supposedly does not understand and instinctively rejects, out of a desire for liberty, the constraints of civilization. The preliminary dialogue between the two Frenchmen obviously outlines a diffusionist model of culture, whereby Western subjects justify colonial expansion in terms of sharing their higher knowledge with less advanced societies. As we will see, Diderot implies that diffusionism could not prove more mistaken, since the most astute cultural wisdom provided in this narrative is not offered by a European, but by Orou, a Tahitian.

The corollary of a diffusionist model of culture, as we have seen, consists of a Eurocentric ontology of human subjects, beginning with the primitive savages discovered in remote parts of the world and ending with European man, the most evolved being on Earth. Through the use of irony and caricaturization, however, Diderot's narrative illustrates that diffusionism is by definition not universal but ethnocentric: that is to say, it takes the customs of one nation and claims that they should be shared by all cultures. As Tsvetan Todorov explains, "ethnocentrism consists in the unwarranted establishing of the specific values of one's own society as universal values. The ethnocentrist is thus a kind of caricature of the universalist."[10] Such a single dialectical understanding of different cultures as simply being the lack of Western civilization is appropriately expressed by means of what could be called a nondialogic dialogue. Characters "A" and "B" are practically interchangeable, engaging in two almost identical monologues rather than a dialogue that expresses different points of view.

Having depicted the false universalism proposed by the two Frenchmen in their monological conversation, Diderot goes on to sketch two clashing ethnocentric perspectives, epitomized by Bougainville and the Tahitian chief. These two monologues also conform to a single dialectical logic. Some critics interpret the chief's attitude as a mark of ethical complexity and even a call for respect among cultures. Most notably, Goodman maintains in *Criticism in Action* that, "The Vieillard's reasoning here takes the following form: (a) You are neither greater nor lesser and are therefore a man. (b) How can you then assert yourself above those to whom you are equal? (c) If we are all men and thus equal, then your right to declare Tahiti as your property implies the Tahitian's right to claim France as his property. (d) You see the absurdity and the injustice of the latter and from there can see that the former must be equally absurd and equally injust" (187). By performing a dialectical reading, I would like to show, however, that the vieillard neither assumes nor proclaims the equality of all men. Instead, like the two Frenchmen, he adopts a single dialectical stance that establishes the superiority of Tahitian society by negating the value of European culture.

The Tahitian leader narrates a "before" and "after" story that establishes a series of juxtapositions between Tahitian and French societies. Before the advent of the French army and their general Bougainville, the chief claims, the Tahitians lived a natural, virtuous, and innocent life. They were at peace with themselves and their environment. This idyllic existence was destroyed by the advent of the Europeans. To the chief, the Europeans represent evil itself. They have traveled to Tahiti only to pillage the country and dominate its people. When the Tahitians bemoan Bougainville's departure, the chief chastises them: "Cry misfortunate Tahitians! cry; but about the arrival, not the departure, of these mean and ambitious men: one day you will know them better" (147).

It is not that the chief is mistaken. With historical hindsight, we know that the Europeans did, indeed, colonize other cultures. Although correct, however, the Tahitian chief allows for no complexity in his vision of the two societies, which he describes in binary terms as the good Tahitian versus the bad European civilization. Even before the Europeans manifested their imperialist intentions, the chief does not know or want to know anything about the Europeans. Readers are told that "Upon the arrival of the Europeans, he cast a glance full of disdain upon them, without showing either surprise, fear, or curiosity. They approached him; he turned his back on them and retired into his cabin" (147). His hatred of Europeans comes not so much from foresight as from prejudice.

The chief's assumptions about European societies, appropriately expressed in a monologue to his people, exactly parallel those of the two anonymous Frenchmen and of Bougainville himself. Both reflect a single dialectical understanding of culture. For these men, the world is divided into two asymmetrical parts: from the Frenchmen's perspective, civilized Europe versus uncivilized non-Europe; from the chief's perspective, pure Tahiti versus corrupt non-Tahiti. Each side establishes the superiority of its own culture by defining the other culture only negatively, as the absence of their own culture. Consequently, as noted, the Europeans praise the rationality, civilization, and morality of Western cultures by depicting non-Western societies as irrational, uncivilized, and immoral. The Tahitian chief follows the same dialectical process to declare cultural superiority. He establishes the innocence, happiness, and morality of his own culture by describing Europeans as their opposites, namely as non-innocent, unhappy and immoral. Starting with such ethnocentric premises, it follows that nothing could be more dangerous for either society than cultural mixture. Cultural exchange, be it economic, social, or sexual, would displace the (single) dialectical structure of us versus non-us and its accompanying hierarchies. As the chief warns his people:

> [W]e are innocent, we are happy; and you can't but destroy our happiness. We follow the pure instinct of nature. . . . Here everything is ours; and you have imparted to us I don't know what kind of distinction between yours and mine. We share our wives and daughters; you enjoyed this privilege with us; you came to stir in them unknown desires. (148)

The binary opposition between Europeans and Tahitians would be incomprehensible without having a common standard of comparison, which could be called, using Marxist terminology analogically, a "general equivalent." By offering a common measure, the general equivalent enables us to assign comparative value to dissimilar entities.[11] In this text, the standard that transcends and measures all cultural differences is provided by what might be called "fraternal patriarchy." Both the French and the Tahitian cultures define ethics in terms of how women are exchanged among men for the purposes of sexual and cultural reproduction.

In emphasizing the role of gender as a general equivalent, I will disagree with Wilda Anderson's argument that reproduction, rather than gender, is what matters most in Tahitian society. According to Anderson, in Tahiti those who can reproduce are valued because they can contribute to the society; those who cannot reproduce are less valued. This interpretation, however, does not explain the androcentrism of the narrative, whereby women are depicted as "owned," shared, and exchanged among men. In Tahiti, as in Europe, women are assumed to be the property of men. As Orou explains to his guest, Tahitian men "share [their] wives and daughters." Relying upon this common cultural foundation, the chief uses fraternal patriarchy to distinguish between the two societies. If women are assumed to be the property and sexual right of all men in a society, as is supposedly the case in Tahiti, then that society is natural and innocent. By way of contrast, if women are regarded as the property of one man, as in European monogamy, then that society is unnatural and immoral. Clearly, insofar as the *Supplément* describes Tahiti to critique France, it criticizes neither a biological definition of sexual difference nor the social inequality between men and women. Instead, Diderot's narrative objects to the particular manner in which the Western patriarchal economy is organized by means of the exchange of women.

If we pursue the logic of both Bougainville's and the chief's monologues, we would be led to the conclusion that the Tahitians attain a better form of civilization because they base their values upon natural sexual difference. Unlike the French, the Tahitians make no mistake about sexual identity. For example, in a brief but significant scene of the *Supplément*, Diderot describes the rape of a female European servant, who was disguised as a man, by a group of Tahitian men. Although the servant's "true sex" had gone unnoticed by the European officers, the more "natural" Tahitians "guess[ed] his gender from the first glance" (152–53). Corrupted by centuries of dissimulation and artifice, the text implies, Europeans can no longer recognize sexual difference. By way of contrast, natural people will immediately perceive sexual identity in the visible, biological, signs of the body.

Literary critics generally stop at this side of the coin, reading the *Supplément* as representing Tahitian culture as ideal and natural to critique Western practices. For example, as Carol Blum argues in *Diderot: The Virtue of a Philosopher*[12]:

> For Diderot, the central virtue of Tahitian culture was not that it liberated from law, that primitive anarchy would be preferable to civilized order, but that the islanders' laws, customs and religion were based upon nature and in harmony with her designs. Unlike the European who was constantly torn between the demands of contradictory authorities, the Tahitian was permitted to experience himself as a whole. The voice of nature and the voice of society were in unison and the word they spoke was: procreate. (121)

Such interpretations of the *Supplément* focus upon the monologic narratives and thus read the entire text according to the logic of the single dialectic. They argue that the *Supplément* contrasts the natural and artificial foundations of society, regarding the Tahitian culture as based on nature and the French culture as its dialectical contrary, namely, as based on lack of natural principles and therefore arbitrary and conventional. Diderot's text, however, is not one sided. At the same time that the author uses gender differences to critique the ethical norms of French culture, I will show, he also uses cultural similarities to critique the Tahitian culture. As we have observed, the chief resembles Bougainville in that he shares a desire to control and manipulate the Tahitian people. By the end of the narrative, most Tahitians reject Bougainville and follow their native leader. In so doing, the text implies, they uncritically exchange one form of ethnocentrism for another.

After showing us how *not* to engage in cultural exchange through a series of single dialectical or monological narratives, Diderot stages a third conversation, between the Tahitian patriarch Orou and the French chaplain, that presents a better model of intercultural communication which pursues the logic of the double dialectic. By all appearances, this conversation resembles the exchanges between Bougainville and the Tahitian chief. As before, fraternal patriarchy provides an appropriate standard by which to measure both cultures because it is the blind spot, or unquestioned foundation, of both societies. Unlike all the other cultural values debated in this narrative, patriarchy is assumed to be universal not only in validity, but also in fact. In making the transition from the single (or monologic) to the double (or dialogic) dialectical narrative, the *Supplément* turns around and represents French culture as the positive term in order to critique Tahitian "nature."

The very circumstances of this third conversation create the possibility for genuine dialogue. Although Orou and the chaplain are still character types, they are dissimilar. In fact, each can be regarded as a spokesman for his society. Furthermore, because the chaplain is a guest in Orou's home, both have the incentive to be polite and open-minded. The crux of the debate between Orou and the chaplain concerns, once again, the issue of which culture implements the best sexual mores. The chaplain claims that his culture, which is based largely on prohibitions—against incest, extramarital, and premarital sex—is superior because it conforms to both human and divine law. Orou pretends not to understand how a divinity could be so removed from human nature as to dictate rules that "prevent one from tasting that innocent pleasure that nature, that sovereign mistress, invites us all to enjoy; to give life to a being that resembles us" (153). Reproduction, he maintains, yields not only personal satisfaction but also general utility since it produces more able bodies for the clan and country. Orou posits that a code of ethics is universal only if it conforms to the following principles: "Do you wish to know what is good and bad everywhere and for all time? Look upon the nature of actions and things; upon your relations to your peers; upon the effect of your behavior upon your personal utility and the general good" (158). Aspiring to the general good and personal utility dictates precisely the ethics observed by

85

the Tahitian people: sharing all women among men; subsuming sexuality to reproduction; and thus imposing absolutely no restrictions upon sexual behavior other than the ones imposed by reproduction itself.

Upon a first glance, the most plausible interpretation of the text is the one offered by Lester G. Crocker in *Diderot's Chaotic Order*,[13] who argues that the *Supplément* confers more value upon the Tahitian, or "natural" view of sexuality over the French, or "cultural" suppression of it. Crocker maintains that "Sexual restrictions foment disorder, since they are ineffective and only promote rebellion by an impulse overwhelming in its power" (80). This reading, however, like the earlier ones I discussed, also presumes a single dialectical textual logic, in which Tahitian nature and European culture are viewed as opposites and one must overrule the other. By way of contrast to such interpretations, I will argue that the dialogue between the monk and Orou more plausibly reveals a double dialectical logic in which two cultures negotiate their understandings of nature in a process of reciprocal social critique.

In Tahiti, Orou explains, there is no incest taboo; no rule against premarital or extramarital sex; no shame attached to single motherhood. On the contrary, a nubile female is considered more desirable if she already has a few children—a sign of her fertility—some of whom are as a result of sexual relations with her own father—a sign of her desirability. Single motherhood is thus not only a right, but also a point of pride: "The birth of a child," Orou elaborates, "is a happy domestic and public occasion: it is a growth of fortune for the household, and of strength for the nation" (161). Despite the wide divergence in European and Tahitian attitudes toward single mothers, however, L'aumônier is able to understand, if not altogether accept, Orou's argument because they adopt a similar androcentric perspective. To them, a welcome child is a male child. As Orou continues to explain, children "represent more arms and hands in Tahiti; we see in him a farmer, a fisherman, a hunter, a soldier, a husband, a father" (161). Furthermore, as Wilda Anderson observes in *Diderot's Dream*, in both cultures, and particularly Tahiti, children are viewed as patrilineal property and "thus are treasured not as persons, but as the source of material riches" (135).

This system of values and hierarchies based upon fecundity implies that no civilization is natural. Tahiti cannot be plausibly viewed, after all, as the dialectical opposite of France. Orou explains as much when he observes that the Tahitians have sexual prohibitions which are, like the injunctions themselves, related to reproduction. A man or woman who is not at the peak of his or her fertility—either because of age or impotence—should not engage in sexual relations. The only vice consists of "The sign of sterility, an innate evil, or the result of advanced age. The woman who takes off her veil and mingles with men, is a libertine, the man who takes off such a veil and approaches a sterile woman is a libertine" (169). For the Tahitians, sexuality needs to be tied to reproduction in order to remain natural and hence moral. Such ethics are an ethics of utility, since the production of children is equivalent to the production of wealth. As Anderson notes, "From the drive to amass wealth, Orou derives a coherent notion of utility, and from utility, a lucid morality. From this same concept of morality, he then derives social rank and status: they are an index of fecundity" (*Diderot's Dream*, 138). Valuing fecundity requires the strict regulation of women's bodies in particular. Gender-based education thus forms "the main object of private education and the most important principle of public moeurs" in Tahiti (163).

Given these cultural values, it makes sense that Orou and his family feel offended when the chaplain refuses to engage in sexual relations with his wife and nubile daughters, all of whom are close to the peak of their fertility. Confronted with a systematic explanation of Tahitian mores, the chaplain responds defensively. He declares that his religion and state forbid him to engage in sexual relations with Orou's daughters and wife. His answer, repeated without further explanation like a refrain, provides a caricature rather than a fair description of French values. His answers fail to address the obvious problems with Orou's arguments, problems which the text nevertheless underscores. For although Orou wants to convince his interlocutor that the Tahitians live in a nonhierarchical, nonnormative and free society, it is rather clear that this society is neither nonhierarchical nor free, but rather determined by gender hierarchies as well as by distinctions based on age and the ability to reproduce.[14]

More important than the chaplain's defense of his own culture, however, is his attitude toward another. Eventually the chaplain gives in to Orou's wishes and, out of respect for Tahitian values, engages in sexual relations with Orou's youngest daughter without ceasing to believe, however, in the validity of his own ethics. The only real dialogue of the *Supplément* thus describes Tahitian and European cultures in terms of a dialectical process of reciprocal critique that negates the possibility of any utopian vision. As Anderson observes,[15]

> The poignant picture of the Tahitian 'natural culture,' of villagers destroyed by Bougainville's sailor's syphilis and their equivalent contamination by European

mores and religion seems at first glance to be a classic Enlightenment—even Rousseauist—denunciation of the corrupting effect of increasing civilization. But against the backdrop of his materialism, Diderot's story takes on a different cast, a much more ambiguous one, and replaces the primitive innocence of Rousseau's noble savages with the shifting and disabused morality of Rameau's nephew. Diderot's salon philosophers, by abandoning utopian visions, whether negative or positive, accede (seemingly paradoxically) to a position superceding the fatalistic determinism associated with materialism. (127–28)

If we perceive the double dialectical narrative logic of the *Supplément*, we are in a better position to grasp the complexity of Diderot's nonutopic ethical vision. More specifically, a dialectical reading illustrates that the text plausibly combines the cultural bias inherent in universalism with the open-mindedness implied by relativism.

Arguably, Orou's argument would not provide the optimal perspective from which to critique French mores, nor would the chaplain's polite yet defensive reaction to his host's values level an effective critique of Tahitian society had Diderot's narrative simply concluded with this exchange. The text supplements this dialogue with yet another conversation between characters "A" and "B." This final exchange allows readers to identify the most valid ethical stance. In their second discussion, the two Frenchmen appear unrecognizable. Rather than sounding like ethnocentrists, they both sound like Orou. As characters "A" and "B" transform their ethnocentrism into an exoticist appreciation of Tahitian society, they subject European mores to the kinds of critiques leveled by Orou.

Not only do the two Frenchmen maintain that their country's sexual prohibitions violate the laws of nature, but also that they are self-defeating: by forbidding most sexual relations, they only enhance desire. To be effective in their criticism of French society, "A" and "B" claim to identify and reject the very basis of French morality: patriarchy itself. In so doing, they depict Tahitian practices as the opposite, meaning as unpatriarchal:

> As soon as a woman becomes the property of man, and furtive pleasure is regarded as a theft, we see the origin of the terms modesty, reticence, *bienséance*; imaginary vices and virtues; in other words, barriers between the two sexes that invite them to violate the imposed laws, and that produce often a contrary effect, in heating the imagination and titillating the desires. (180)

The root of sexual prohibitions, the Frenchmen concur with Orou, consists of regarding women as the sexual property of men. As we have observed, however, this is precisely the way women are represented in Tahitian culture. After all, fraternal patriarchy provided the common standard that enabled these men to debate the relative merits of European versus Tahitian societies. By replacing one version of patriarchy with another, Diderot's narrative exposes the limits, if not impossibility, of imagining the supposed universal ethics it idealizes in Tahitian culture: one, that is, that respects the natural rights of all human beings. While beginning to imagine a distinctly modern ethics that values autonomy, by using patriarchy as a general equivalent that assesses the merits of each culture, the text undermines its own objective.

The *Supplément* does not leave us empty-handed, however. In his depiction of several voyages from Europe to Tahiti, Diderot is able to offer both positive and negative models of cultural exchange. The successful traveler, the author suggests, is one who reconciles what he may consider to be the universalist values of his own culture with the relative values of another. Characters such as the Tahitian leader and Bougainville are never able to see beyond the supposed universalism of their own culture. Both assume that only their values are correct. Paradoxically, this cultural chauvinism has the textual effect of relativizing the universal, since it represents universalist ethics as a form of blind ethnocentrism. By way of contrast, Orou and the chaplain are open-minded enough to engage in mutually beneficial dialogues about the validity of their moral beliefs.

In the conclusion, one of the Frenchmen urges readers to have a modest attitude toward their own ethics and a tolerant one toward those of others: "Let's imitate the good monk: monk in France, savage in Tahiti" (186). The Frenchman thus suggests that only individuals who can question the ethical norms not only of different cultures, but also their own, gain a truly ethical consciousness that benefits from cultural exchange. The *Supplément* transforms the general Enlightenment question "should we civilize man?" into an open-ended discussion about what constitutes civilization and which forms of it are best suited for different peoples. While not resolving the impasse between relativist and universalist ethics, the text offers a good start by presenting generations of critical readers with a model of dialogue that functions as the basis of a double dialectical, and thus more reciprocal and less hierarchical, understanding of cultural difference.[16]

CHAPTER FOUR

Notes

1. See, for example, the arguments presented by Edward Said in *Orientalism: Western Representations of the Orient*.
2. The translations of passages from Diderot's *Supplément* are my own.
3. For more information concerning the complex interrelations Diderot establishes between sexuality and ethics, see Wilda Anderson's *Diderot's Dream*.
4. As Pierre Saint-Amand aptly poses this question in *The Laws of Hostility: Politics, Violence, and the Enlightenment*: "It is not difficult to understand how the incommunicability of cultures subsequently becomes the main subject of Diderot's book. Indeed, the *Supplément* is a theorization of passage from one place to another and of the possibilities of all forms of exchange.... Are we condemned to the impossibility of exchange, to the untranslatability of mores and languages?... Do we have eyes only to see no further than ourselves, bounded as we are by our cultural narcissism?" (123).
5. As Dena Goodman observes in *Criticism in Action: Enlightenment Experiments in Political Writing*: "Diderot's *Supplément au Voyage de Bougainville* extended the critical project inaugurated by Montesquieu, but in a direction radically different from the one pursued by Rousseau in the *Second Discours*.... In Diderot's hands, the dialogue became an extension of Montesquieu's comparative critical method, an extension that transformed criticism into a method for social and political reform. The activity of the reader which had been stimulated by the epistolary text could be redirected into the world through dialogue. For the dialogue, as Diderot conceived it, became a model of active reading, and reading critically, the model of analysis to be applied to all laws and institutions" (170).
6. As Wilda Anderson argues in *Diderot's Dream*, "the order in which the reader encounters the various scenes is crucial. Each scene provides the ethical framework in which to situate and therefore to interpret correctly the text that follows.... A framing dialogue between two European philosophers in a French garden begins the text, links the embedded dialogues, and wraps up the discussion at the end. The first embedded dialogue presents the Tahitian patriarch's speech.... The second, the best-known part of the *Supplément*, presents the dialogue that had taken place several weeks earlier between a European monk and a Tahitian father and natural philosopher, together with the interpolated story of an ethically astute prostitute from the American colonies" (129).
7. In *Diderot: Le Labyrinthe de la Relation*, Saint-Amand explains the reasons behind Diderot's critique of the theoretical sciences, most staunchly defended by d'Alembert, and preference for the experimental sciences.
8. As Tsvetan Todorov indicates in *On Human Diversity: Nationalism, Racism, and Exoticism in French Thought*, because the exotic is often equated with one's own cultural ideals, it cannot be attributed to a well-known culture, since familiarity with the shortcomings of that society might preclude idealization. Exoticist dis-

course thus depends upon a dissatisfaction with one's own culture combined with a vague and distant knowledge of another culture upon which one projects one's own fantasies.

9. For an analysis of the manner in which natural historians used "primitives" and women to understand more advanced societies, see Ludmilla Jordanova's *Sexual Visions: Images of Gender in Science and Medicine between the Eighteenth and Twentieth Centuries* and Londa Schiebinger's *The Mind Has No Sex? Women in the Origins of Modern Science.*

10. Todorov, *On Human Diversity*, 1–2.

11. The concept or metaphor of the general equivalent describes the manner in which certain cultural objects or qualities are extracted from the market of symbolic goods and invested with an absolute rather than comparative value. This process, in turn, enables those goods or qualities to function as a measure of the value of other goods.

12. Blum, *Diderot: The Virtue of a Philosopher*, 121.

13. See Lester G. Crocker's *Approach to Synthesis*. Princeton: Princeton University Press, 1974. *Diderot's Chaotic Order.*

14. As Anderson observes in *Diderot's Dream*, "The Tahitians view their society as being in equilibrium with nature—or better, they feel that they have realized an ideal, the creation of a fixed social structure that accommodates the changeability of the natural world. Notice that their culture does have a directional development of a sort. It must have been more egalitarian years before; it becomes relentlessly more hierarchized as the years go by, according to the principle of a single-parameter meritocracy. The Tahitians, however, do not perceive this vector" (141).

15. See Anderson's *Diderot's Dream.*

16. As Goodman observes in *Criticism in Action*, "In this rhetoric can be seen a new form of politics, a politics not based on the authority of the absolute but one whose means—and perhaps even whose end—is reasoned discourse and whose authority is common sense. . . . And the agents of this reform, the critical politicians, are the critical readers themselves, the enlightened public that had been created by fifty years of philosophic and critical activity" (226).

CHAPTER FIVE

Hybridity and Ethics in Chateaubriand's *Atala*

The figure of the noble savage constitutes one of the defining features of French Romanticism. As contemporary criticism points out, this figure is riddled with ambivalence. While savage cultures may epitomize an innocent state of nature by way of contrast to a dissolute Western civilization, they also represent a less developed social organization that makes Western societies appear superior by comparison. Rousseau's works perhaps best capture the philosophical ambivalence of early Romantic representations of savage cultures.[1] On the one hand, Rousseau praises the supposed moral innocence of the noble savage. He regards this figure as the origin of Western civilization before it became corrupted by private property and the greed, artifice, and despotic governments that developed as a result of it. On the other hand, Rousseau maintains, the noble savage cannot be considered either moral or immoral.[2] Rather than making ethical choices between good and evil, he is motivated by both positive (or other-regarding) and negative (or selfish) impulses.[3] As Rousseau indicates in *Discours sur l'origine et les fondements de l'inégalité parmi les hommes* (1755), only civilized man has the potential to function as an autonomous and group-oriented moral and political being who interacts on a par with other citizens in a republican society.[4] Consequently, Rousseau's seemingly paradoxical representation of the contrast between nature and civilization—whereby he simultaneously praises and deprecates the noble savage—depends upon a binary normative model.

From one perspective, Rousseau's ethical vision may appear nuanced and even impartial. Both civilized and savage people are capable of positive and negative sentiments; both can engage in good and bad actions.

CHAPTER FIVE

From another perspective, however, it is clear that only civilized man can be judged good or evil; the noble savage is simply amoral. The true opposition established by Rousseau is therefore not, as it would seem, between the virtue of nature and the evil of culture or vice versa, but rather between the applicability of normative standards to culture and their irrelevance in nature. The notion of civilized man—be he depicted as good, evil, or a mixture of both characteristics—entails, quite literally, the negation of the amorality associated with the state of nature. Otherwise put, the savage represents the lack of morality. Because only the ethical status of civilized man matters, the noble savage acquires an admittedly instrumental function in Rousseau's works.[5] Rather than being an object of study in itself, as Rousseau himself indicates, the noble savage is a hypothetical model employed to imagine the origin of Western civilization and to identify errors in its moral development.

While Rousseau may be the best-known philosopher of the early Romantic dichotomy between nature and culture, Chateaubriand gives this distinction its most popular literary voice.[6] Unlike Rousseau, however, in his descriptions of the contrast between "l'homme sauvage" and "l'homme civilisé," Chateaubriand is concerned with the moral status of both. He assumes that, whatever their differences may be, so-called civilized and primitive societies are not ethical opposites.[7] The recognition of all cultures as forms of civilization may be attributed, in part, to Chateaubriand's travels throughout the world. More specifically, in 1791 Chateaubriand visited North America. Upon his return to France, he wrote a travel narrative that he subsequently transformed into the novels *Atala* (1801) and *René* (1802).[8] *Atala* in particular, I will argue, challenges a representation of Western and Native American cultures as ethical opposites. While beginning *Atala* with the familiar contrast between savage nature and European culture, by the end of the novel Chateaubriand transforms this polarity into a more complex model of *hybrid* cultural identity. What does the concept of hybridity entail and how is it formed? To address this question, it is necessary to take a detour into contemporary theory. Thus, before turning to *Atala*, I will set up the theoretical framework of my argument by explaining how both modern and contemporary texts share a dialectical, or "hybrid," model of cultural identity.

In *Colonial Desire*, Robert Young traces the genealogy of the "hybrid" from its botanical, zoological, and anthropological origins during the eighteenth and nineteenth centuries to its contemporary use in postcolonial criticism as a trope of subversion of colonial discourse. Young observes that eighteenth-century discourse employed the term "hybrid" to describe a biological grafting together of different plants to the point where their difference is no longer discernible. During the nineteenth century, the term hybridity acquired racial connotations by referring to the union of different species or races understood as opposites. In both cases, according to Young, hybridity "describes a dialectical articulation" (23). He elaborates:

> At its simplest, hybridity ... implies a disruption and forcing together of any unlike living things, grafting a vine or rose on to a different rootstock, making difference into sameness. Hybridity is a making one of two distinct things, so that it becomes impossible for the eye to detect the hybridity of a geranium or a rose.... Hybridization can also consist of the forcing of a single entity into two or more parts, a severing of a single object into two, turning sameness into difference.[9]

What does Young mean by depicting the formation of hybrid identity as "dialectical"? Let us unpack this statement. As criticism on the subject of race demonstrates,[10] in colonial discourse racial categories are produced by means of a process of negation that begins with a Western subject who is assumed to be the standard of humanity. This subject acquires specific cultural characteristics by rejecting (or negating) the qualities associated with other, non-Western subjects.[11] To offer a typical example, the category of a "rational" Western subject is created by negating irrationality from its definition and projecting that quality upon a non-Western subject. In this semiotic relation, the non-Western subject has no identity of its own acquired, in turn, by means of the negation of Western characteristics. Colonial discourse therefore utilizes what could be called a "single dialectical process" to depict non-Western subjects as nonsubjects.

The goal of reaching a pure Western subject by means of a dialectical process of negation of non-Western characteristics, however, is doomed to failure. In fact, reading cultural identity in terms of the dialectic leads us to acknowledge the fundamental *hybridity* of cultures. When one culture requires the exclusion of qualities associated with another culture to create its own semiotic and national boundaries, the excluded culture becomes part and parcel of its own definition. In depending upon the negation of other cultural identities, it stands to reason that the category of "us" simultaneously incorporates the concept of "non-us" or "them." If we pursue the logic of the dialectic, we are led to the conclusion that the categories "us" and "them" used to draw racial, ethnic, or national distinctions are not only semantically interrelated, but also inseparable.[12] In other words, insofar as it depends upon a dialectical articulation, cultural identity is inherently hybrid.

So far, however, we have only examined one kind of hybridity, achieved by means of a single dialectic, whereby two cultures are positioned in hierarchical and oppositional relations to each other. This observation raises the following question: is there a way of conceptualizing cultural relations without relying upon a dialectical model suitable for describing only cultural hierarchies? In other words, how are more symmetrical power relations between different cultures formed? This is precisely the line of inquiry pursued by contemporary postcolonial scholarship.

Twentieth-century criticism that addresses the subject of race has identified the problems inherent in conceptualizing the relationship between Western Self and non-Western Other as a single dialectic. Nonetheless, as Young observes, by regarding racial categories as unchangeable, the criticism of Sartre, Fanon, and Memmi, for example, "has constructed two antithetical groups, the colonizer and the colonized, self and Other, with the second only knowable through a necessarily false representation, a Manichean division that threatens to reproduce the static, essentialist categories it seeks to undo" (5). Cultural contact and fusion, Young maintains, follow a more complicated semiotic process that unsettles such binary racial categories. According to Young, by way of contrast to early twentieth-century criticism, contemporary theory employs the concept of hybridity to challenge both the notion of harmonious intercultural unity and that of absolute cultural distinctions.[13]

Edward Said, for instance, notes that in a dialectical relationship between two "opposite" cultures, races or societies,

> Hybridity . . . becomes a third term which can never in fact be third because, as a monstrous inversion, a miscreated perversion of its progenitors, it exhausts the differences between them. This doubled hybridity has been distinguished as a model that can be used to account for the form of syncretism that characterizes all postcolonial literatures and cultures.[14]

What does Said mean by describing hybridity as "a third term," "a monstrous inversion," and "doubled"? I believe that he is taking the dialectical process that produces racial categories in colonial and even postcolonial discourse a step further than his theoretical predecessors, most notably Sartre and Fanon. In so doing, Said literally doubles the single dialectic. We have already seen that a single dialectic describes hierarchical relations between "us" and "non-us." To reiterate, such a model traces the semiotic process whereby one group acquires a positive identity by negating the qualities that it projects upon another group.

By way of contrast, a doubled dialectic traces the semiotic process whereby two groups acquire cultural identity by excluding from their self-definition qualities that are associated with a so-called "opposite" group. Because the double dialectic describes relations of reciprocity, it shifts away from a paradigm of cultural identity that revolves around a Western subject. Indeed, as contemporary critics justifiably point out, postcolonial societies do not represent themselves only in terms of lacking Western characteristics, as a single dialectical model of culture would suggest. Insofar as they differentiate themselves from the West, postcolonial societies do so in order to establish what could be called a "positive identity"—that is to say, their own cultural characteristics. The fact that two cultures—let us say, for example, a former colony and a former colonial power—define themselves in opposition to each other does not, of course, necessarily imply that they have equal power once decolonization takes place. It does suggest, however, that despite a potential difference in power, they both regard themselves as unique and important societies in their own right. The double dialectic is thus particularly appropriate for mapping out both the hierarchical and the nonhierarchical relations between cultures which define our postcolonial world.

In addition, the double dialectic depicts a process of cultural mixture that poses a challenge to models of cultural purity. As noted, the dialectic depicts the process whereby two cultures that are regarded as opposites simultaneously negate and incorporate the qualities associated with their counterparts. In so doing, the double dialectic outlines a semiotic process of cultural mixture or hybridity. If we assume cultures to be inherently hybrid, however, are we led to the conclusion that we have reached a postmodern era beyond cultural identity? Even those scholars who are most sympathetic to the deconstruction of identity respond with caution. Young, for example, identifies the continuities between what could be called the single dialectical models of culture that characterize colonial discourse and double dialectical ones:

> Hybridity in particular shows the connections between the racial categories of the past and contemporary cultural discourse: it may be used in different

ways, given different inflections and apparently discrete references, but it always reiterates and reinforces the dynamics of the same conflictual economy whose tensions and divisions it re-enacts in its own antithetical structure. (27)

Clearly, Young cautions, the hybrid is not a utopic (or dystopic) concept beyond race, ethnicity, or other forms of identification. On the contrary, the dialectical process of forming a hybrid identity illustrates that even a fusion of two cultures does not eliminate their differences, as a facile understanding of the dialectic as a process of thesis-antithesis-synthesis would suggest. Rather, by simultaneously incorporating and negating select qualities of its component cultures, a hybrid culture simultaneously preserves and cancels the difference between them.

We are therefore led to conclude, along with Young, that the concept of hybridity—be it understood as an asymmetrical power relation between two societies (as in the single dialectic) or as a potentially symmetrical one (as in the double dialectic)—"shows that we are still locked into parts of the ideological network of a culture that we think and presume that we surpassed" (27). Having described the two ways in which relationships between cultures can be conceptualized in terms of the dialectic, let me now turn to the second line of inquiry pursued by this essay: namely, how does an understanding of culture as intrinsically mixed provide some viable ethical solution to the impasse between universalism and cultural relativism? More specifically, *Atala* considers the following problem: if we assume that no culture is pure, what are the ethical implications of cultural hybridity upon the manner in which different societies represent and interact with each other?

The novel provides an illuminating answer to this question by depicting the relationship between the allegorical figures of Chactas, a Natchez who was raised by a Spanish general, and Atala, an American Indian princess, who, as it turns out, is the natural daughter of that general. I call the characters of Atala and Chactas "allegorical" because they clearly represent more than two Romantic figures coping with the consequences of Spanish colonialism. Chateaubriand uses the ethnically mixed characters of Atala and Chactas to reflect upon the ethical implications of any colonial ventures, anticipating France's own expansion under the Napoleonic empire.[15] The clashes between two radically different cultures, which are manifested on a psychological level in the moral struggles of Chactas and Atala, raise the following, more general, questions: is Europe's own civilizing mission ethically justified? If so, on what grounds? Is cultural union possible in a colonial context? If so, what form would it take? This essay will examine how *Atala*[16] observes a dialectical narrative process to lead from an understanding of identity as *hybrid*[17] to what could be called an ethics of cultural complexity, which assumes that no society is either evil or ideal.

The novel begins with a prologue that expresses a nostalgia for the Spanish colonial period. "France once possessed, in seventeenth-century America," the narrator informs us, "a vast empirre that spread from Labrador to Florida, and from the Atlantic coast to the furthest lakes of northern Canada" (39). The middle part of North America appears, at the outset, not only as the absence of the advanced culture represented by colonial Spain, but also as the lack of any civilization whatsoever. America, in other words, represents an empty wilderness. The nostalgia for empire is thus cast not in terms of conquest of other societies, but rather in terms of the civilized man's return to the purity of nature.[18] Nature symbolizes the universal cradle of humanity, an Eden where civilized man may rediscover his lost innocence: "Yet grace is always wedded to magnificence in nature's scenes," continues the narrator (40). "[W]hile the middle current carries with it the corpses of pines and oaks, we can see on the two lateral currents floating islands of pistia and waterlilies" (40). No sooner has the narrator sung this *éloge* to an unpopulated, nurturing nature that lacks any signs of civilization, however, than he anthropomorphizes the natural scene. Nature no longer symbolizes the absence of civilization. Instead, it mirrors the opposition between the two cultures that populate the North American territory: the Orient and the Occident.

Correspondingly, nature adopts the supposed characteristics of its inhabitants on each side of the river that divides the North American territory. On the Spanish side, the lush, orderly and prosperous landscape invites a proprietary and admiring glance "on the vastness of its waves and the savage abundance of its shores" (41). The Oriental side of the river displays features that are the very contrary of the Occidental natural environment. "Such is the scene on the occidental shore," the narrator pursues, "but it changes on the opposite side, and takes on the form of a striking contrast" (41). On this side, nature is disorderly, entangled, blending incongruously yet beautifully a vast array of wild trees and flowers to create an enticing palette of colors and odors: "Suspended on the streams of water collected on the rocks and on the mountains, dispersed upon the valleys, trees of all shapes, colors, and

CHAPTER FIVE

odors intertwined and grew together, climbing to heights that tired the glance" (41).

Chateaubriand's description of the animal kingdom dramatizes the same striking contrast between Orient and Occident as the vegetation:

> All is silence and calmness in the savannas of the other side of the river, here, on the contrary, all is movement and murmur: beaks hitting tree trunks, the steps of animals . . ., the noise of waves, feeble cries, . . . sweet sounds filled these deserts with a tender and savage harmony. (42)

The polarization between Occident and Orient (or civilization and savagery) delineated by the description of the natural environment conforms, I would argue, to the logic of the single dialectic. That is to say, the text begins with a description of the Occident and represents the Orient only as its negation. According to this paradigm, if the Occident is orderly, then the Orient is disorderly; if the Occident is calm and quiet, then the Orient is frenetic and noisy. The Occident thus acquires cultural characteristics only insofar as it excludes certain qualities—such as disorder and noise—that are projected upon the Orient. I intend to show, however, that *Atala* begins with this binary opposition between Occident and Orient only to set up the single dialectical model of culture, which it will subsequently undermine and double.

Indeed, the characters who populate this polarized setting are the products of cultural mixture. Chactas, for instance, has not only been brought up by a Spanish father and an American Indian mother, but also has lived in both Europe and North America. In a fast-paced biographical introduction, readers are informed that Chactas was:

> Detained in prison in Marseille by a cruel injustice, freed, introduced to Louis XIV; he conversed with the great men of the century and attended the balls at Versailles, Racine's tragedies, Bossuet's orations, in a word, the Savage had contemplated society at the pinnacle of its splendor. (43)

Clearly, Chactas is both insider and outsider to European society. Initially perceived as an outsider and enemy by the French, he was arrested and imprisoned. At the same time, when it served French colonial interests, Louis XIV regarded Chactas's hybrid background as a useful liaison between France and North American Indian tribes and consequently invited him to Versailles.

Impressed with the splendor of European courts as much as he is disappointed by their despotism, Chactas displays an ambivalent attitude toward Europe, combining criticism and respect. Based upon his life experiences, Chactas ultimately decides to regard each culture as composed of a series of relatively unique individuals rather than as a homogeneous and unified mass. At the same time, he only identifies one virtuous Frenchman—Fenélon—among many who are unjust.[19] Based upon this particular example, "Despite the numerous injustices suffered by Chactas from the French, he loved them. He always remembered Fénelon, whom he hosted, and wished he could be of service to the compatriots of this virtuous man" (38).

Understanding culture as both ethnically mixed and ethically complex, Chactas implies, does not involve either denying cultural differences or blurring the moral distinction between good and evil. Chactas invokes the trope of the chiasmus to explain to René the dialectical process that transformed both of them into hybrid individuals: "It's a singular destiny, my dear son, which unites us. I see in you the civilized man who became a savage; you see in me the savage which the great Spirit . . . wished to civilize" (47). What does Chactas mean by describing their destiny in terms of the chiasmus? As is well known, in poetics, the figure of the chiasmus refers to a structure in which elements are repeated in reverse. Employing this figure as a dialectical scheme, Chactas regards himself and René as ethnic inverses. Whereas René rejected (or negated) his European heritage to acquire a Native American identity, Chactas rejected (or negated) his Native American identity to become Europeanized. Clearly, the chiasmic inversion between Chactas and Atala only makes sense if one assumes Native American and European identities to be semantic and cultural opposites. That is, the distinction between men like René and men like Chactas depends upon a process of reciprocal negation, which I have called a double dialectic. Producing European identity—or the attributes of "l'homme civilisé"—requires eliminating the qualities associated with "l'homme sauvage" and vice versa.

Despite its reliance upon binary distinctions, the logic of the double dialectic undermines the stereotypical contrast between "l'homme civilisé" and "l'homme sauvage" that it initially creates. First, as mentioned, the very opposition between civilized and savage men requires selective incorporation. The concept of civilization semiotically necessitates, and thus includes, the negation of the concept of the savage and vice versa. Second, and perhaps more importantly, Chactas both incorporates and negates elements of his American Indian heritage to become Europeanized. Similarly, René both incorporates and negates elements of his European heritage to become Native American.[20] This process of mutual negation and selective incorporation of opposing qualities therefore obscures, without completely eliminating, cultural differences. In so doing, the double dialectic creates what I have called hybrid individuals and societies. Because they assimilate and reject elements of two distinct cultures, hybrid individuals aquire a unique vantage point from which to understand and criticize both their own and foreign societies: "Having entered life by means of two different paths," Chactas remarks, "you came to rest in my place, and I came to sit in yours; thus we must have had two totally different perspectives on things" (47).

Chactas's reflections concerning the inverse paths pursued by himself and René disclose yet another advantage of understanding the formation of cultural identity as a double dialectic. As we have seen, such a process of reciprocal negation and incorporation of given cultural characteristics between savage and civilized men does not have to imply hierarchy. In a double dialectical relationship, both cultures are taken as "positive terms"—meaning concepts that acquire meaning by eliminating characteristics associated with their cultural opposites. Assuming the European and Native American cultures to have equivalent value, Chactas identifies the advantages of hybridization without, however, deciding who—himself or Réne—has benefited most from cultural mixture. He thus concludes the description of the chiasmus (or double dialectic) with the genuinely open question: "Who, you or me, has gained or lost most in this change of place? Only the Spirits know, among whom the least knowing has more insight than all men put together" (47).

Chactas's personal history further explains how he came to regard cultures as intrinsically hybrid. At seventeen years of age, we are told, Chactas and his father fought for the Spanish against several Indian tribes. In that battle, Chactas was injured and his father was killed. The young man was subsequently found by the Castilian general Lopez who treated him like a son and educated him to appreciate both American Indian and Spanish cultures. Although he respected both societies, Chactas initially regarded them as dialectical opposites. In his estimation, Spanish culture excluded the natural life of Natchez society and, conversely, savage life excluded any form of civilization. After visiting Spanish cities, however, Chactas began to endow this binary opposition with normative implications. He became increasingly disenchanted with his European heritage and longed to obliterate all traces of Western education: "Not being able to resist the need to return to the desert," he recalls, "one morning I appeared before Lopez, dressed in my Savage clothes, holding in one hand my bow and arrow and in the other my European clothes. I returned them to my generous protector and kneeled before him while crying torrents of tears. I called myself horrible names and accused myself of ingratitude: 'Yet after all, I said to him, o my father, you can see it yourself: I will die if I do not return to my life as an Indian'" (49). His father replies: "'Go... child of nature! Regain this independence of man that Lopez does not want to deprive you of'" (49). By framing the distinction between Spanish and Natchez cultures as a contrast between the constraints of civilization and the freedom of nature, Chactas and Lopez appear to follow Rousseauistic stereotypes.

The implied narrator, however, treats such distinctions with irony. For instance, shortly after his visit to Europe, Chactas gets captured by two rival tribes whose members enchain and plan to sacrifice him. Despite this horrific experience, in the beginning young Chactas continues to idealize Native American cultures, claiming, in a manner that calls to mind Rousseau's famous aphorism "Man is born free and everywhere he is in chains," that he prefers savagery in chains to freedom in civilization. Chactas declares:

> Even though I was a prisoner, the first few days I could not help but admire my enemies. The Muscogulg tribe, and even more so its ally the Seminole tribe, breathes happiness, love and contentment. His gait is light, his glance open and serene.... Even age cannot destroy in the Sachems this joyous simplicity; like the old birds in our woods, they still blend their old songs with the new tunes of their young posterity. (50)

Even as he praises Native American cultures, however, Chactas observes European stereotypes. Adopting the binary opposition between Seminole nature and European culture, he regards all Indian tribes as unified by the same natural demeanor and way of life.[21] According to his idyllic description, nature is not only a part of the American Indian environment. The Native Americans represent the mirrors of nature, living freely as the birds in the trees, preserving and transmitting their "joyous simplicity" from generation to generation.

As in Rousseau's works, so in *Atala* gender oppositions play an important role in drawing the boundaries between nature and culture. In

Europe, Chactas observes, gender differences are obscured by artifice. By way of contrast, in the Seminole tribe women epitomize the very qualities that men lack. While the men are silent and unsympathetic to his plight, the women seem concerned about his fate, ask many questions about his feelings and past, and feel moved by his praises: "These praises very much pleased women," Chactas notes approvingly. "[T]hey showered me with all sorts of gifts; they brought me nut cream and sugar, . . . bear meat, . . . soft grass for my bed. They sang, they laughed with me, and afterwards they began to cry, thinking that I would be burned" (51).

No sooner has Chactas considered himself American Indian as opposed to European, however, than he finds out that being Native American—or, as he puts it, "sauvage"—does not entail a homogeneous and unified identity. The Seminole men prepare for his sacrificial ritual. Likewise, despite their show of sympathy, the Seminole women abandon the young prisoner to his fate. In retrospect, Chactas bemoans the human condition to René, stating: "Woe to mankind, my dear son! These same Indians whose customs are so touching; these same women who had shown such a tender interest in me were now asking for my sacrifice; and whole nations postponed their departure for the pleasure of seeing a young man suffer horrible torments" (67).

Among all the American Indians of the rival tribe, only one person perceives Chactas as a kindred spirit: the Seminole chief's beautiful daughter, Atala. She lays aside her feelings of loyalty to both tribe and family in order to free Chactas and guide him away from danger. One would expect that Chactas would be grateful to Atala for saving his life. Surprisingly, this is not the case. Once freed, the young man claims to prefer bondage to freedom:

> How incomprehensible are mortals moved by passion! I had just abandoned the generous Lopez; had just been exposed to all sorts of dangers to be free; and in a second the glance of a woman changed my desires, my resolutions, my thoughts! Forgetting my country, my mother, my home and the horrible death that awaited me, I became indifferent to all that was not Atala. Without the strength to elevate myself to man's reason, I had fallen all of a sudden in a kind of childlikeness. (57)

Chactas's apparently contradictory reaction becomes comprehensible once we observe that at this point in the narrative gender becomes Chactas's main way of establishing dialectical cultural distinctions. After being freed by Atala, Chactas no longer considers European culture as the representative of civilized bondage and American Indian culture as the representative of natural freedom. Now both European and Native American cultures come to represent masculine freedom in contradistinction to the emotional bondage inherent in his love for Atala. Consequently, while cultures become particularized, gender roles become universalized. All the important elements of Chactas's existence—his culture, family, and values—begin to signify the lack of Atala who, by way of contrast, becomes a figure of universal plentitude.[22] Despite this shift in attitudes, however, at this point in the narrative Chactas obviously continues to rely upon a (single) dialectical model of identity: one that regards femininity as the negation or absence of masculine characteristics.[23] In his estimation, Atala represents an ethereal, emotive, and quasi-divine being that is the very opposite of the self-reliance and rationality that he associates with masculinity.

While being Chactas's foil in terms of gender roles, however, Atala mirrors his cultural background. Like Chactas, Atala is a hybrid. She is born of an American Indian mother and a Spanish father, who, as noted, is none other than Lopez himself. Influenced by her dual heritage, Atala fosters a deep sympathy for American Indian and European cultures that is tempered only by her criticism of both societies. She considers herself simultaneously pagan and Christian, blending and confusing the two traditions in her sacrilegious love for Chactas. Atala describes herself as "proud like a Spaniard and like a Savage. My mother made me a Christian so that the God of my father would also be my God" (81). Although Atala's education may have been intended to subsume the Native American tradition into the Christian one, this goal was not reached. It soon becomes clear that, rather than either effacing one tradition or combining two distinct heritages, Atala selectively incorporates and rejects elements of both cultures.

On the one hand, Atala's effort to save Chactas's life reflects her critical stance toward the American Indian rituals of sacrificing captured enemies. By helping Chactas escape, we could say that she negates important elements of her tribe's ethics. Adopting European ideals, she not only proclaims the superiority of private love over public war, but also, and more importantly, the sanctity of human life. In addition, considering herself Chactas's sister, Atala refuses to marry him in part because of her reluctance to violate the incest taboo. On the other hand, Atala also rejects (or negates) European values. Despite her passionate love for Chactas, Atala poisons herself in order to be able to keep the promise of chastity made to her mother. By attempting to keep her vow, Atala intends to manifest her loyalty to the American Indian culture, to which her mother belonged. At the same time, her very refusal of marriage and promise to remain chaste represent an attempt to follow Christian rather than Seminole ethics. To complicate this chiasmic inversion even further, Atala's adherence to her native heritage indicates a misguided loyalty to the Christian religion. Which is to say, her mother bargains with God, in a rather un-Christian fashion, to preserve her daughter's chastity in exchange for saving her life.[24] By poisoning herself to keep her filial promise, Atala thus not only fulfills a misconstrued obligation but also violates Christian ethics in disposing of her own life.

Perceptively, Chactas describes Atala's moral contradictions as a tension between maternal and paternal values, which interact, but never harmoniously blend in her moral character: "The perpetual contradictions between love and religion in Atala, her tender abandon and the chastity of her values, the pridefulness of her character and the depth of her sensibility, the nobility of her spirit in all great things, her susceptibility to all the small ones, all of this made her an incomprehensible being to me" (75). Chactas claims not to understand Atala's moral struggles. His perceptive analysis of her personality, however, points to his identification with her divided loyalties. Like Atala, Chactas constantly oscillates between espousing and rejecting both Western and American Indian values.

For instance, after fleeing from captivity with Atala, Chactas begins to feel disappointed by American Indian practices. He thus rejects (or negates) elements of his native culture and, like Atala, turns for solace and guidance to the other side of his heritage: namely, the Catholic faith of his father. Both Chactas and Atala become greatly influenced by a Christian missionary, Père Aubry, who hides the lovers in his abode to protect them from the pursuing Seminole Indians. The young couple immediately notices that Père Aubry's hands had been mutilated, as it turns out, by members of an American Indian tribe. When Chactas and Atala express outrage at this act, the missionary replies, "If the Indians hurt me, they are misfortunate blind beings that God will illuminate one day" (88). Under his influence, Chactas perceives Christianity as a universal religion, capable of adapting to and improving any society.

Nonetheless, true to his hybrid upbringing, Chactas is not prepared to forsake his American Indian roots. Like Atala, he wishes to combine the best elements of both societies to create a superior ethics, albeit one deeply influenced by the Christian religion. Commenting upon the lifestyle of a small group of Indians who had converted to Christianity, Chactas exclaims:

> Oh, the charm of religion! Oh, the magnificence of the Christian creed! In the place of sacrificed an old monk, for altar a stone, for church the desert, for aid innocent Savages. . . . There reigned the most touching mixture of social and natural. . . . I admired the triumph of Christianity over savage life; I saw the Indian become civilized at the voice of religion; I witnessed the primitive union between Man and Earth. (94–95)

Chactas continues to regard American Indian and European cultures as the products of mutual negations: the former symbolizing nature, the latter civilization. This vision of cultural synthesis—one which, according to my reading, corresponds to a misunderstanding of the dialectic of cultural formation as a process of union of opposites—is nonetheless short-lived. Chactas becomes disillusioned with both cultures once he sees that combining two cultures does not necessarily lead to the peaceful and harmonious life he had envisioned.[25] After he finds out that Atala has poisoned herself to obey what she (mis)understood to be a Christian vow, Chactas abruptly changes his mind about the universality of Christian ethics and its applicability in all contexts.[26] He exclaims: "Just look at this much-praised religion! Perish the sermon that steals Atala from me! Perish the God that goes against nature! Man-priest, what did you come to do in these forests?" (101). Père Aubry explains that Christian morality did not dictate that Atala obey the vow of chastity. He observes that, had Atala properly understood Christian morality, she and Chactas could have married and led a blessed and happy existence.

Père Aubry's message, however, as well as the apologia for the ethical superiority of Christian over savage life, remains unpersuasive.[27] Unlike the more explicitly polemical *Génie du Christianisme* (1802),[28] *Atala* conveys a more contradictory and even pessimistic attitude toward the possibility of establishing any ethical standards as universal. Instead of offering an *a priori* and generally applicable normative system, *Atala* outlines a dialectical narrative process that advises a critical attitude toward all cultural standards.[29] This questioning of values, which has been associated with *le mal du siècle*, however, should not be equated with nihilism. Rather than rejecting value, *Atala*'s main characters epitomize and encourage the search for lasting, or at least meaningful, moral standards that can function as the basis for a good life. Their failure to reach absolute answers does not imply that the quest is meaningless itself.

On the one hand, Chactas's and Atala's cultural hybridity—their often incongruous mixture of Native American and Western beliefs—motivates the fatal plot of the novel. On the other hand, despite this classically tragic ending there is also an overwhelmingly positive side to Chateaubriand's allegorical representation of identity as mixed and internally divided. An understanding of cultures as hybrid discourages efforts to purify cultures of their others or to propose any cultural identity as ideal. In addition, *Atala* changes the Rousseauistic connotations of the concept of the noble savage. For if no society is the model of perfection and, furthermore, if all people, even so-called savages, are considered capable of ethical judgment and error, then all societies and people are subject to both internal and external ethical evaluation. Once we assume the ethnic and ethical hybridity of culture, the idealization of any society—be it one's own or another—becomes as difficult as its complete deprecation.

Notes

1. See Jacques Derrida's analysis of Rousseau's aporia between the primacy and superiority of nature versus that of civilization in " . . . That Dangerous Supplement," *Of Grammatology*.

2. In *Discourse on the Origin of Inequality*, Rousseau traces the development of civilization in terms of three distinct stages: the state of nature, the transitional period of the Golden Age, and different kinds of civilizations that emerge with the notion of private property. He imagines that in the state of nature human beings are driven by egocentric rather than social impulses while still feeling pity for the suffering of their fellow men: "At first it would seem that men in that state, having among themselves no type of moral relations or acknowledged duties, could be neither good nor evil, and had neither vices nor virtues, unless, if we take these words in a physical sense, we call those qualities that can harm an individual's preservation 'vices' in him, and those that can contribute to it 'virtues'" (34–35).

3. In the *Discourse on the Origin of Inequality*, Rousseau argues that only during the Golden Age, the period when human beings invented tools, built dwellings, and cultivated crops, did they depend upon each other sufficiently to unite into groups and foster moral feelings. By way of contrast, primitive men lived isolated and amoral lives. Rousseau paints the following picture of primitive humans: "Let us conclude that, wondering in the forests, without industry, without speech,

without dwelling, without war, without relationships, with no need for his fellow men, and correspondingly with no need to do them harm, perhaps never even recognizing any of them individually, savage man, subject to few passions and self-sufficient, had only the sentiments and enlightenment appropriate to that state; he felt only his true needs, took notice of only what he believed he had an interest in seeing; and that his intelligence made no more progress than his vanity" (41).

4. Rousseau regards Geneva as the paradigm of an ethical republican civilization while identifying aristocratic France as the paradigm of corrupt civilization.

5. In the *Discourse on the Origin of Inequality*, Rousseau openly acknowledges that his description of the state of nature is an explanatory myth or, at best, an educated hypothesis: "[I]t is no light undertaking to separate what is original from what is artificial in the present nature of man, and to have a proper understanding of a state which no longer exists, which perhaps never existed, and probably never will exist, and yet about which it is necessary to have accurate notions in order to judge properly our own present state" (10–11).

6. *Atala* was a huge and immediate success. As Richard Switzer documents in *Chateaubriand*, *Atala* was supposed to be published as part of the larger work, *The Genius of Christianity*. Instead, the author decided to publish *Atala* sooner and separately. The appearance of *Atala* transformed Chateaubriand from an unknown to a famous author. "Thus it was," observes Switzer, "that in 1801 appeared *Atala*, an 'Indian' tale vaguely inspired by his travels in America and by his readings. . . . There are not many examples of such immediate and total success of a work of literature as in the case of *Atala*. From a penniless émigré hiding behind an assumed name, Chateaubriand suddenly became the proverbial toast of Paris literary society" (29).

7. Chateaubriand expresses this opinion even more emphatically in *Travels in America*, stating: "From the examination of these languages alone, it is clear that the peoples named by us as savages were far advanced in that civilization which involved the combination of ideas" (120).

8. See Tsvetan Todorov's more detailed description of Chateaubriand's travels to America and discussion of their possible literary and philosophical implications in *On Human Diversity: Nationalism, Racism and Exoticism in French Thought*.

9. Young, *Colonial Desire: Hybridity in Theory, Culture and Race*, 26.

10. As David Theo Goldberg observes in *Racist Culture: Philosophy and the Politics of Meaning*, during the eighteenth and nineteenth centuries, "primitive societies were theorized in binary differentiation from a civilized order: nomadic rather than settled; sexually promiscuous, polygamous, and communal in family and property relations rather than monogamous, nuclear, and committed to private property;—illogical in mentality and practicing magic rather than rational and scientific" (155).

11. We can therefore state that the racial categories produced by colonial discourse emerge from a dialectical relation where only the Western subject functions

CHAPTER FIVE

as a "positive term." That is to say, only the Western subject acquires a specific cultural definition by rejecting the qualities of its non-Western "Others."

12. As Robert Young notes, "Fixity of identity is sought only in situations of instability and disruption, of conflict and of change . . . In each case identity is self-consciously articulated through setting one term against the other" (4).

13. For example, Homi Bhabha uses the term hybridity to indicate the textual moments where colonial discourse subverts its own authority. More specifically, in "The Commitment to Theory," the term hybridity describes moments of counterauthority that dismantle various binary hierarchies between Self and Other constructed along the lines of race, class, or gender. Bhabha refers to "the 'hybrid' moment of political change," stating: "Here the transformational value of change lies in the re-articulation, or translation, of elements that are *neither the One* (unitary working class) *nor the Other* (the politics of gender) but something else besides which contests the terms and territories of both" (13).

14. Edward Said, *Culture and Imperialism*, 24–25.

15. The sociopolitical questions raised by *Atala* are not far removed from Chateaubriand's political interests. As Richard Switzer explains in *Chateaubriand*, "Historically, Chateaubriand played important roles in three areas. In the political world he was an ambassador, cabinet minister, and statesman, and his many pamphlets in support of the principle of legitimate monarchy made him one of the outstanding supporters of the French legitimate monarchy. Except in America, where the different conditions allowed little comparison with France, Chateaubriand had slight experience with democracy, and he shared the ideas of the eighteenth-century theorists who found in the constitutional monarchy the ideal form of government" (ii).

16. This chapter has appeared in *Nineteenth-Century French Studies* (Fall, 2001). All references to *Atala* are to the 1971 Gallimard edition. The translations of passages into English are mine.

17. As Jean-Pierre Richard notes in *Paysage de Chateaubriand*, the figure of the hybrid character is prevalent in Chateaubriand's allegorical fictions: "Different blood, intermixed blood, we always encounter the syncretic image of the *hybrid*. But what will be its destiny? Will the hybrid succeed in maintaining without drama the mediating function which its nature leads it to assume?" (143). As Richard continues to answer his own question, "Nothing seems less certain. All of Chateaubriand's fictions seem to lead to the disastrous nature of métissage" (143, my translation). In agreement with Richard, I will argue that Chateaubriand uses hybrid characters to provoke thought about the problems of cultural difference rather than to provide facile solutions.

18. As Richard Switzer argues in *Chateaubriand*, the author does not idealize America univocally: "In a more strictly literary field, Chateaubriand's two other important roles came to the fore. In 1791 Chateaubriand traveled to America, and although there is evidence that in many ways he was disappointed by what he

saw in the New World, he became, through his many writings dealing with America, one of the foremost interpreters of America to the European public in the early nineteenth century" (ii).

19. As Carlos Lynes argues in *Chateaubriand as a Critic of French Literature*, "A strong Rousseauistic note is sounded here as Chactas expresses his disillusionment with French civilization and as he hastens to leave the hut. . . . In this mood, Chactas calls upon Fénelon, who succeeds in reconciling him with men and society by showing the brighter side of the picture in such a way that society, with all its flaws, seems to the Indian better than the state of nature" (16).

20. The novel *René* confirms Chactas's description of their life paths as chiasmic, or the negation of two opposing terms. While Chactas follows a dialectical process that leads him to respect both European and Native American cultures, René is too saddened by his personal experiences to appreciate either.

21. As Gilbert Chinard notes in *L'exotisme américain dans l'oeuvre de Chateaubriand*, "A la base même de l'exotisme, se trouve en effet un désir éternel d'échapper à son temps, à la civilisation qui nous entoure, de changer de milieu" (vi).

22. The universalization of the figure of Atala, which becomes so abstract that it is virtually emptied of content, is carried to an extreme by the conclusion of the novel, when Atala is reduced to a lifeless corpse that symbolizes self-sacrificial femininity. As Naomi Schor observes in the chapter "Triste Amérique: Atala and the Post-Revolutionary Construction of Woman" of *Bad Objects: Essays Popular and Unpopular*: "By making the lifeless corpse of the young Indian maiden an allegory of Virginity, Chateaubriand successfully manages to capitalize on the legitimating power of female allegory, while voiding the feminine form of female corporeality and desire and erasing from it the marks of racial difference. The allegorization of woman, a sort of degree zero of female representation, can only be brought about through a violent act of suppression of all particularities, not to mention life" (147).

23. I would agree with Schor's interpretation in "Triste Amérique" that, ultimately, Atala becomes a figure of femininity that helps pave the way for the reactionary sexual (post)revolutionary regime that consolidates a strict division of spheres and excludes women from the public sphere. At the same time that *Atala* "founds the tradition of representing woman in the nineteenth-century as sexually stigmatized," however, it also blurs gender distinctions to illustrate, by means of the similar experiences of Atala and Chactas, both the limits and promises of cultural mixture. (138)

24. Although, as Schor notes in "Triste Amérique," "the language of the mother is coextensive with that of the Christian apologist," I would argue, against much criticism on the subject, that Chateaubriand does not use the figures of Chactas, Atala, or her mother to rehabilitate Christianity or to synthesize harmoniously Christian and pagan life. Rather, if we follow the dialectical movements of

the narrative, we arrive at the conclusion that the text finds both the neat distinction between pagan and Christian and their reconciliation problematic, if not impossible (143).

25. Some critics plausibly relate this disillusionment to the *mal du siècle* that Chateaubriand expresses much more in *René*. Switzer, for instance, describes this literary and even philosophical attitude in *Chateaubriand*: "At that point in which the desires and the passions of the individual have developed, but before these passions can be satisfied, there occurs this intermediate and confused state in which the individual does not know himself, cannot analyze his sentiments, cannot bring any remedy to his melancholy—all this for no reason that he can fathom" (48).

26. In *Chateaubriand: Composition, Imagination, and Poetry*, Charles Porter regards this normative ambivalence as the result of Chateaubriand's mixed narrative strategies: "It seems to me plain that Chateaubriand originally set out to write *Atala* as a demonstration of the havoc wreaked on the state of nature by the encroachments of civilization, in particular by ill-understood or poorly-proclaimed Christianity. Then, having decided to use *Atala* as an example of the 'harmonies de la religion' . . . , he found himself constrained to . . . transform its message. From this shift remains a most uneasy diffusion of interest in the story" (82).

27. Although in many of his works Chateaubriand attempts to offer Christianity as a moral solution to political and social problems, the logic of his texts repeatedly undermines such a solution. For instance, *Le Génie du christianisme* (1802) attempts to illustrate that only religion can satisfy man's quest for meaning. Yet the two most famous novels of *Le Génie*, namely *Atala* and *René*, undermine the possibility of any solace, be it religious or secular, and give voice instead to the inconsolable *mal du siècle*.

28. Published in 1802, this text examines the history, art, and architecture of Christianity to reconsolidate its influence following the French Revolution. In so doing, *Génie* both anticipates and contributes to the growing influence of the Church during and following the reign of Napoleon I.

29. Todorov correctly points out in *On Human Diversity* that the dialectical process which yields moral standards in *Atala* does not involve a simple synthesis between the radically different values of European and American Indian cultures, but rather a selective incorporation and negation of elements of both cultures: "And yet Chactas's ideal, like Chateaubriand's, [is] not to embrace the life of society (and its highest form, Christian life) without reservation, but rather to attempt a synthesis between the good aspects of each state" (292).

CHAPTER SIX

The Dialectical Process of Decolonialization: Fanon's *The Wretched of the Earth*

If the wealth of current postcolonial scholarship that addresses the subject of cultural relativism offers any indication, the impasse between universalist and relativist ethics constitutes one of the most pressing problems examined by contemporary postcolonial criticism. To even begin to find an equilibrium between intercultural respect and critique, however, requires cultures to be on a more or less equal footing. As postcolonial critics point out, colonialism precludes such ethical reciprocity. Frantz Fanon was one of the first philosophers to identify this impossibility.[1] In 1961, he voiced what seemed at the time a radical proposition. Fanon claimed that "... decolonization is always a violent phenomenon.... It is quite simply the replacing of a certain species of men by another species of men" (35). Without a doubt, *The Wretched of the Earth*[2] was a revolutionary book both politically and philosophically.[3] It not only called for violent revolution against colonial powers, but also explained why a reversal of positions between colonizer and colonized was conceptually necessary to the process of decolonization.

The identities of the settler and native, argues Fanon, are constructed by means of a dialectical process. Only by negating the humanity of the natives through the use of violence, geographical segregation, deprecatory discourse, and economic exploitation could settlers represent themselves as the universal standards of humanity. In other words, the exclusion of those declared as inhuman creates the semiotic boundaries of the fully human. Furthermore, because settlers establish superiority by excluding the natives from definitions of humanity, universalist appeals to an all-inclusive human identity and standards of justice fall on deaf ears.

CHAPTER SIX

Consequently, the only way for the settlers to overcome the dialectical negation of their identity and culture, Fanon suggests, is by enacting a reversal of values and power that dehumanizes the settlers in turn. In the simultaneous process of denying the humanity and incorporating the power of the settlers, natives regain their national identity and cultural pride.

For obvious reasons, however, Fanon and future postcolonial critics have remained dissatisfied with this reversal of positions between colonizer and colonized, or more generally, to use Todorov's apt terminology, between "us" and our "Others."[4] A (single) dialectical model of cultural relations, though descriptive of a colonial context, cannot capture the more complicated power dynamics of a postcolonial world. The question then becomes: is there a way of conceptualizing potentially nonagonistic relations between cultures without reverting to a universalist model of human identity which is, in its very essence, defined by means of a dialectical process of exclusion of other societies or cultures?[5] Otherwise put, what is a possible solution to the impasse between theoretical models that postulate endless cultural conflict and those that assume an impossible human unity? Several postcolonial critics, including Fanon himself, Edward Said, Homi Bhabha, and Robert Young have proposed conceptual models that not only describe the processes of colonization and decolonization, but also attempt to find ways of overcoming the binary hierarchies they institute. This essay will analyze and evaluate Fanon's attempt to describe and possibly overcome what I will call a single dialectical model of cultural identity: one, that is, where the identity of one culture is established by negating (and, usually, devaluing) the qualities of another.

In *The Wretched of the Earth,* and more specifically in the chapter "Concerning Violence," Fanon demonstrates that colonialism depends upon a single dialectical process. Only by representing natives as inferior, or inhuman, argues Fanon, can settlers claim to embody the universal standards of humanity. An alien in his own land and relegated to the status of nonperson, the native has no hope of declaring his equality without resorting to violence. "National liberation, national renaissance, the restoration of nationhood to the people, commonwealth: whatever may be the headings used or the new formulas introduced," Fanon famously announces, "decolonization is always a violent phenomenon" (35). It would be a mistake, however, to see Fanon solely as an apostle of violent revolution. As much as he argued for the necessity of violence, he imagined a world ruled by peaceful relations among cultures. Influenced by a confluence of intellectual movements and historical events, including Marxism, existentialism, Freudian psychoanalysis, and the Algerian War of Independence, Fanon integrated all of these cultural currents into a theory that combined the violent process of liberation with a hope for peace. His dialectical theory of cultural identity thus offers not only a model for understanding social inequality in a colonial context, but also for possibly transcending it. In both respects *The Wretched of the Earth* remains highly pertinent to discussions of ethical models in a (post)colonial context.[6]

As a student of Sartrean existentialism, psychoanalysis,[7] and Marxist materialism,[8] Fanon was drawn to the explanatory powers of the dialectic. Indeed, the dialectic has been employed by philosophers ranging from Hegel to Fanon to describe a historical and conceptual process that is intended to achieve progress through a series of sublations. A sublation refers to the operation by which a being or culture progresses to a superior stage by simultaneously incorporating some of the positive qualities and eliminating some of the negative qualities of its former stage of development. A dialectical process generally requires several sublations before attaining its goal. This teleological process explains how beings and societies can reach a supposedly perfect state by overcoming gradually their deepest problems and realizing their inherent potential.[9] Observing the Hegelian model, Fanon explains that the dialectic of decolonization represents not only a conceptual but also a "historical process: that is to say, that it cannot be understood, it cannot become intelligible nor clear to itself except in the exact measure that we can discern the movements which give it historical form and content" (36).

Just as Hegel postulates that the unrealized essence of being is rationality, so Fanon assumes that equality and mutual respect among cultures constitute the unrealized potential of human civilizations. Such potential, as noted, can only be achieved once humanity moves through several dialectical stages of history. Contrary to what humanist discourses maintain, Fanon argues, societies cannot pass from colonial oppression to a postcolonial era without undergoing a process of decolonization that requires violence:

> Decolonization never takes place unnoticed, for it influences individuals and modifies them fundamentally. . . . It brings a natural rhythm into existence, introduced by new men, and with it a new language and a new humanity. Decolonization is the veritable creation of new men. (36)

CHAPTER SIX

Unpacking this statement, we observe that Fanon outlines three main dialectical stages that transform modern societies: (a) a colonial period characterized by the dehumanization of the native by the settler; (b) a revolutionary period that necessitates the dehumanization of the settler by the native by means of strategies such as violent revolution, rejection of colonial values, reversal of power, and myth and magic; and (c) a postcolonial period during which human beings negate all cultural partialities—including ethnocentrism, religious fundamentalism, or extreme nationalism—and incorporate the value of all societies. Let us now follow the steps of Fanon's dialectical process of decolonization in order to explore the fruitful models of cultural interaction it offers.[10]

Colonialism, or the Dehumanization of the Native by the Settler

Colonialism positions native and settler in a nonreciprocal dialectical relationship in which the former establishes superiority by denying the humanity of the latter. To undo this relation of power and reclaim his humanity, the native must resort to violence and dehumanize the settler in turn. "Decolonization," Fanon explains,

> is the meeting of two forces, opposed to each other by their very nature, which in fact owe their originality to that sort of substantification which results from and is nourished by the situation in the colonies.... In fact, the settler is right when he speaks of knowing "them" well. For it is the settler who has brought the native into existence and who perpetuates his existence. (36)

Fanon is not simply making the obvious point that the settler would not exist as such without the colonial system. He is also explaining that settler and native become semiotically and historically inseparable in their dialectical opposition.[11] The settler, whom we will call "subject A," acquires his identity and power only by excluding the native, who then becomes "subject non-A," from definitions of humanity. The settler depends upon, and therefore partially incorporates, the identity of the native in order to acquire, by way of contrast, his self-definition.[12] The identity of the settler can be described as a hybrid semiotic and cultural formation composed of an identity he tries to exclude (the native, the Other) that makes possible the one he creates (the settler, myself). Because the settler represents the native as a nonperson to glorify his own culture, Fanon can claim that the settler "has brought the native into existence."[13] Without imposing a colonial regime that depicts the native as his cultural opposite, the settler could not be a settler.

The topography of the colonized territory further distinguishes settler and native. "The colonial world," Fanon notes, "is a world cut in two. The dividing line, the frontiers are shown by barracks and police stations" (38). The distinct zones inhabited by settlers and natives are not, however, established through a process of *reciprocal* exclusion since "the zone where the natives live is not complementary to the zone inhabited by the settlers" (38). In other words, the relation between settler and native, or subjects A and non-A, is clearly single dialectical. While the settler acquires his identity by segregating the native and labeling him less than human, in the absence of revolution, the native acquires no independent definition in turn by excluding the settler. As Fanon emphasizes, "The two zones are opposed, but not in the service of a higher unity" (39). Those who envision a possible reconciliation between settler and native without the need of overthrowing the colonial powers, Fanon suggests, are not simply politically misguided, but also conceptually mistaken. They fail to understand that when one identity is formed only through the negation of the other, "No conciliation is possible, for of the two terms, one is superfluous" (39). To attempt to reconcile a human (the colonialist) with a nonhuman (the native) on equal terms, Fanon argues, would be to fail to see the inherent hierarchy between colonizer and colonized. This naive desire for the union of opposed forces, Fanon further implies, also points to a misunderstanding of the dialectic as process that leads to a simple synthesis of opposites without radical change (or the elimination of undesirable qualities).

Fanon repeatedly emphasizes that negation constitutes a necessary step of the historical and conceptual process of decolonization. Only reversing the logic of colonialism can transform the native from a nonentity, or what Fanon calls "the thing which has been colonized," into a human being. That is to say, only what could be called a double dialectical process of mutual exclusion could lay the foundation for a more egalitarian postcolonial world. By denying the humanity of the colonialist, the native takes a first step in regaining his dignity and self-worth. In the struggle for national independence, which sets him in opposition to the colonizer, the native becomes the first term (or subject B) whose human identity is determined by the exclusion of the nonhuman qualities associated with the settler (or subject non-B). Now the settler acquires a negative, or derivative, identity by being defined as the negation of the native. As during colonialism, in the process of decolonization the identity of the settler becomes inextricably connected to that of the native. Both colonizer and native represent hybrid subjects who define themselves by simultaneously excluding and incorporating each other's cultural characteristics.[14] While this doubled dialectic may not lead to harmonious relations between native and settler, it provides the starting point for eventual peace. Without first overcoming colonial hierarchies, Fanon indicates, peace is just another excuse for maintaining colonialism. "In decolonization," he observes, "there is therefore the need of a complete calling in question of the colonial situation. If we wish to describe it precisely, we might find it in the well-known words: 'The last shall be the first and the first last'" (37).

Reversal: (Double) Dialectical Strategies of Decolonization

Basing his theory in part upon his observations of French colonization of Algeria and his personal involvement in the Algerian Revolution,[15] Fanon suggests that there are many possible ways of attempting to reverse colonial power, such that at least in the colonized territory, "The last shall be the first and the first last." Not all of the means of changing the single dialectical structure of colonialism into a double relation between two cultures are equally successful. Nor are all of them necessary steps for decolonization. Nonetheless, Fanon observes, colonized nations tend to adopt at least some of the following dialectical strategies of revolt: (a) envy or desire to reverse positions with the colonialists; (b) local compromises with the colonialists; (c) rejection of Western values; (d) reversion to native religious traditions involving myth and magic; and (e) violent revolution against the colonial power. Employing the conceptual scheme outlined so far, we could say that Fanon assesses the success of each of these strategies of decolonization in terms of how effectively they double the logic of the single dialectic process that helped institute colonialism.

Envy

In the colonial context, the settlers seem to have it all. There is a striking contrast between colonizers and colonized, the haves and have-nots.

The natives live in poor huts, starved, and without proper clothing. The settlers, on the other hand, own large and beautiful houses, eat abundantly, live in luxury. From the perspective of the native, the colonizers have everything desirable. Hence, it is not surprising that, "The look that the native turns on the settler's town is a look of lust, a look of envy; it expresses his dreams of possession—all manner of possession: to sit at the settler's table, to sleep in the settler's bed, with his wife if possible. The colonized man is an envious man" (39). To say that the native is envious is also to suggest that he is defined negatively, as a lack: the lack of power, food, proper shelter and clothing, value and respect. The native's envy is a symptom of the inhuman status to which he has been reduced by colonialism. "And this the settler knows very well," Fanon continues, "when their glances meet he ascertains bitterly, always on the defensive, 'They want to take our place.' It is true, for there is no native who does not dream at least once a day of setting himself up in the settler's place" (39). In his desire to exchange positions with the settler, the native wishes to reverse colonial power, understood both as a political occupation and as a dialectical operation that denies his humanity, thereby transforming the settler into the epitome of the human. In his envy, the native dreams of much more than acquiring colonial goods or luxuries. He desires nothing less than to reclaim his lost dignity, nation, and power.

If he acts upon envy alone, however, the native will not accomplish his ultimate goal. By acting upon his desire to be like the settler, the native may negate colonial power, but he will also incorporate colonial values. In so doing, the native will remain a nonself. Envy alone cannot complete the dynamics of a double dialectic whereby the native acquires a positive self-definition by negating, and thus distinguishing himself from, the settler. In other words, envy traps the native in a single dialectic that establishes the identity of the colonizer as superior. In so doing, it only reinforces the assumption that the colonialist epitomizes the model of humanity which the native should strive to emulate.

Compromise

While envy represents the poor man's dream of overcoming colonialism, compromise functions as the bourgeois's strategy. Rather than wishing for a reversal of power between himself and the settler, the bourgeois native desires to pair up with the colonialist as an equal in exploiting the native masses. The native elite has many reasons for wanting to maintain colonial power. The colonial system enables them to earn their livelihood as factory owners, doctors, teachers, and lawyers. Although accepting colonial values, the elite nonetheless proposes to change the hierarchical structure between colonial and native that relegates it to the same nonhuman status as the masses. The bourgeoisie thus asks for equal rights in an inherently unequal society. In their dream of equality, Fanon suggests, the elite, like the envious masses, misconstrues the workings of the dialectic as a stable synthesis of opposites:

> The intellectual who for his part has followed the colonialist with regard to the universal abstract will fight in order that the settler and the native may live together in peace in a new world. But the thing he does not see, precisely because he is permeated by colonialism and all its ways of thinking, is that the settler, from the moment that the colonial context disappears, has no longer any interest in remaining or in co-existing. (45)

The blindness of the native elite, Fanon suggests, results from its ambivalent subject-position in relation to colonialism. Being relatively privileged within the colonial system, they have incorporated too many of the European values (language, culture, education, class status) and negated too few. They fail to understand that by definition "settler" and "native" are engaged in an asymmetrical relation whereby the former acquires his identity only by exploiting and dehumanizing the latter. By cooperating with the colonial system, the native elite undermines the process of decolonization (44).

The native elite's hopes for equality are not as vain, however, as the poor man's envy. When the natives are completely oppressed, the colonizers do not differentiate between rich and poor, educated and noneducated natives. To them, "the indigenous population is discerned only as an indistinct mass," a dehumanized non-us (44). Once the native population begins to rebel, however, the settlers look for allies in the ranks of the native elite. Thus, "during the period of liberation, the colonialist bourgeoisie looks feverishly for contacts with the elite and it is with this elite that the familiar dialogue concerning values is carried on" (44). During the first phase of decolonization, Marxist dialectical materialism intersects with the dialectics of (de)colonialism. Up to this moment, the Marxist dialectic between bourgeois and worker functions mostly analogically to Fanon's dialectic. Although the two processes may operate in similar ways, they describe distinct phenomena. "It is neither the act of owning factories, nor estates, nor a bank balance which distinguishes the governing classes," as far as Fanon is concerned (44). Under colonialism, "The governing race is first and foremost those who come from elsewhere, those who are unlike the original inhabitants, 'the others'" (44). The exclusion of certain peoples from definitions of humanity on the basis of their race, nationality, or culture initially motivates the dynamics of colonialism.

Just as for Marx human identity is defined in terms of ownership (capitalist, or subject A) or lack of ownership (worker, or subject non-A) of the forces and means of production, so for Fanon identity is defined in terms of belonging or not belonging to a given race. At the point where class alliances form between natives and colonialists, however, the Marxist dialectic ceases to have only analogical explanatory powers. It becomes clear that "In the colonies the economic substructure is also a superstructure. The cause is the consequence; you are rich because you are white, you are white because you are rich" (44). Consequently, when colonialists find it in their best interest to cooperate with the native elite, the dialectics of race and class become indistinguishable. A revolution must therefore accomplish two main objectives. It must negate colonial power while at the same time minimizing, if not altogether eliminating, class distinctions. Only by doubling the dialectics of class and race can the native masses hope to regain their humanity.

Rejection of Western Values

To overcome colonialism, the native masses must first reject the values shared by the colonialists and native elite: namely, the model of so-called universal humanity that defines them as nonpersons; as beings not worthy of being treated ethically. By way of contrast to the native elite's call for equality,

> The natives' challenge to the colonial world is not a rational confrontation of points of view. It is not a treatise on the universal, but the untidy affirmation of an original idea propounded as absolute. The colonial world is a Manichean world.... As if to show the totalitarian character of colonial exploitation the settler paints the native as a sort of quintessence of evil. Native society is not simply described as a society lacking in values, but also the negation of values. (41)

The native masses come to realize that the colonial values they desired represent a hollow universality. The settlers postulate the superiority of their own culture. They declare that Western values should be imposed upon the rest of the world by means of colonial expansion. Rather than being applicable to all human beings, colonial values establish authority through a process of exclusion and denigration of most of humanity. Once he becomes aware of this ruse of universalism, Fanon declares, "in revenge, the native laughs in mockery when Western values are mentioned in front of him" (44).

At this point, the native completely reverses his feelings of envy and desires instead to purify his culture of all traces of colonialism. Because the type of universalism that justifies colonial expansion offers an ethnocentric ethics, the native reasons, so must all other Western values, which now "seem like collections of dead words; those values which seemed to uplift the soul are revealed as worthless, simply because they have nothing to do with the concrete conflict in which the people is engaged" (47). The native now rejects the colonial language, the nuclear model of the family, the Judeo-Christianity religion, and, above all, the individualism that, in his estimation, has prevented his people from uniting against the colonial power. "The very forms of organization of the struggle will suggest to him a different vocabulary. Brother, sister, friend—these are the words outlawed by the colonialist bourgeoisie," that become his means of self-definition not as an isolated being, but as a member of a nation fighting for independence (47). These terms give the native a worthy goal as well as a positive identity. Once he negates colonial values, the native no longer perceives himself as a nonhuman and his culture as a lack of (Western) civilization. Does this rejection of colonial values pave the way for the creation of two free and independent societies? In other words, has the native succeeded in transforming a single dialectical relation between himself and settler into a double dialectical relation between two equals? Not completely. The logic of Fanon's text suggests that, by defining himself only as the opposite of the settler, the native continues to depend upon the colonial identity to create his self-definition. His identity is a hybrid of rejected colonial qualities and his own, culturally opposite, characteristics. Because of his hybrid identity, the native will not be able to return to his precolonial identity. Just as a purified past is irretrievable, so is an autonomous future. As long as the natives set up the colonialists as enemies in order to gain an oppositional sense of national identity, they cannot achieve cultural independence.

Myth and Magic

As we have seen, colonialism justifiably fills the native with a sense of anger, dread, hostility, and awe toward the occupying power. Once he has rejected Western values, Fanon observes, the native does not want to admit his fear of Western domination. The seat of colonial power is removed from his field of vision; the settlers who surround him are only local functionaries. Thus, even before engaging in armed struggle, the native desires to combat the mysterious source of colonial authority, which gains strength as it recedes in distance. One way the native overcomes his fears, Fanon explains, is by attributing them to another source, a source deeply rooted in his own society. Rather than standing in awe of colonial power, the native displaces both his feelings of fear and violence upon his own community. He reverts to traditions which unleash such emotions in "[s]ymbolical killings, fantastic rites, imaginary mass murders" and other rituals that "reveal themselves as essentially personal" (56). As a result, "the settler's powers are infinitely shrunken, stamped with their alien origin. We no longer really need to fight against them since what counts is the frightening enemy created by myths" (56).

Along with the wholesale rejection of Western values, the reversion to native rituals endows the native with a distinct identity. He no longer represents the opposite of Western man, but a person integrated "in the traditions and the history of [his] district or of [his] tribe" (56). By believing in the supernatural, the native incorporates his feelings of anger and awe toward colonialism, but negates the real source of these sentiments. As is the case with the previously discussed strategies, there are advantages and drawbacks to this return to atavistic traditions. On the one hand, as noted, denying the power of the settler endows the native with a distinct identity that "reassures [him], it gives [him] a status, as it were an identification paper" (56). On the other hand, engagement in magical rituals dissipates the native's energies in a struggle against imaginary powers, diverting him from his real goal of overcoming colonialism. In addition, the denial of colonial power observes the same dialectical process as the rejection of Western values. By establishing native identity as the opposite of colonial identity, the reversion to myth and magic renders the native dependent upon (the incorporation and negation of) colonial values. The native and colonizer therefore remain hybrid entities whose identities are intertwined by a process of reciprocal exclusion. To sever this bond, Fanon suggests, the natives must first uproot colonialism from their land through violent revolution and rebuild their lives and nation independently of colonial culture.

CHAPTER SIX

Violent Revolution

Overwhelmed by colonial oppression, the natives eventually confront the real problem of colonialism. As Fanon notes:

> During the struggle for freedom, a marked alienation from these practices is observed. . . . After centuries of unreality, after having wallowed in the most outlandish phantoms, at long last the native, gun in hand, stands face to face with the only forces which contend for his life—the forces of colonialism. (58)

During this phase of decolonization, the native incorporates the resentment and hatred he feels for colonialism but negates their illusory expression. He thus "discovers reality and transforms it into the pattern of his customs, into the practice of violence and into his plan for freedom" (58). Based upon his experience as a psychiatrist, Fanon believes that violence has a cathartic effect upon the natives. It not only unites them toward a common cause, but also unleashes their repressed emotions. For these reasons, the author argues, violent revolution is necessary for mending the broken subjectivity of the people and consolidating the strength of the nation: "The mobilization of the masses, when it arises out of the war of liberation, introduces into each man's consciousness the ideas of a common cause, of a national destiny, and of a collective history" (96). As we have observed, once the natives revolt, the settlers attempt to divide them against themselves into antagonistic classes and tribes. By way of contrast, revolution unites all the natives against the colonial power in a common nation. The colonialists and natives now become engaged in a reciprocal, or double dialectical, process of negation that positions both groups on a more equal footing. Initially, there is no avoiding this mutual antagonism, Fanon explains. Only decades or even centuries after decolonization can both sides hope to rebuild their lives without setting themselves in opposition to each other.

The Utopic Phase: The Negation of Partiality and Incorporation of All Humanity

The era beyond reciprocal exclusion constitutes the utopic aspect of Fanon's postcolonial vision. Like most utopic visions, however, this one as well is barely outlined. Although Fanon's dream of a peaceful world may be vague, however, his dialectical theory remains precise. During this last phase of the process of colonialization and decolonialization, the native and colonizer no longer exist as such. All exclusionary cultural partialities are negated—be it in the form of nationalism, fundamentalism, chauvinism, or ethnocentrism—and the equality of all peoples is incorporated into a new model of universal humanity. Insofar as both the single and the double dialectics have depended upon the negation of another culture to uphold one's own cultural values, this last dialectical step dismantles the dialectic. Nations and peoples no longer define themselves through mutual exclusions that devalorize other societies. For this utopic vision to materialize, Fanon maintains, former colonial powers must cease to demonize their former colonies and vice versa:

> What [the Third World] expects from those who for centuries have kept it in slavery is that they will help it to rehabilitate mankind, and make man victorious everywhere, once and for all. . . . This huge task which consists of reintroducing mankind into the world, the whole of mankind, will be carried out with the indispensable help of the European peoples, who themselves must realize that in the past they have joined the ranks of common masters where colonial questions were concerned. (106)

When *The Wretched of the Earth* pursues the dialectical process of colonialization and decolonialization to its conclusion, it reverts to the very universalist form of relativism that it originally criticized. Although Fanon argues for the necessity of revolution and reversal, he longs for a world that is no longer divided into masters and slaves; one that respects all human cultures. He imagines such a world in the last phase of the dialectical process of decolonization. Perhaps hundreds of years after decolonization, he suggests, "a new race of men" will inhabit a postcolonial world that has negated all cultural partiality and incorporated the value of all human beings. Such a conceptual solution to the impasse between models of cultural homogeneity and those of irreconcilable difference is both useful and problematic. While Fanon's new universalist vision precludes judging one culture as superior to another, it also discourages potentially valid cultural criticism.

Fanon's dialectical theory of colonialism and decolonization thus leaves us with the same seemingly insoluble ethical problem with which his work began: namely, how to respect cultural diversity without lapsing into an empty universalism that levels differences and precludes critique.

CHAPTER SIX

Once all cultural practices are incorporated into a dialectical vision of the universally human, it becomes difficult to see how some practices and actions, including genocide, war crimes, political oppression, can be justifiably criticized. Thus, on the one hand, while noting the narrowness of Western universalism, Fanon cannot avoid proposing a utopic vision that suffers from the opposite flaw: namely, that of being too broad to provide a useful ethical model for cultural critique and interaction. On the other hand, Fanon's postcolonial vision is as pragmatic as it is utopic. Although it may be difficult to imagine a world that respects all cultural differences, in an era of international nuclear, chemical, and biological armament it is equally difficult to imagine humanity continuing to exist without such a world. Contemporary postcolonial theory, I believe, inherits Fanon's hope and challenge: that of creating an ethical model that encourages both respect and criticism among radically different cultures.

Notes

1. For introductions to Fanon's thought and life, particularly his political theories and Marxist influence, see David Caute's *Frantz Fanon*, Peter Geismar's *Fanon* and Irene L. Gendzier's *Frantz Fanon: A Critical Study*.

2. I will be citing from the Grove Press Edition translated by Constance Farrington. The original book, *Les damnés de la terre*, was published by François Maspero Editions, 1988.

3. For discussions of Fanon's political thought, see Marie B. Perinham's *Holy Violence: The Revolutionary Thought of Frantz Fanon, an Intellectual Biography* and Jack Woddis's *New Theories of Revolution: A Commentary on the Views of Frantz Fanon and Regis Debray and Herbert Marcuse*.

4. See Tsvetan Todorov's typology of universalist and relativist theories in *On Human Diversity: Nationalism, Racism and Exoticism in French Thought*.

5. As Robert Young observes in *Colonial Desire: Hybridity in Theory, Culture and Race*: "Since Sartre, Fanon and Memmi, postcolonial criticism has constructed two antithetical groups, the colonizer and the colonized, self and Other, with the second only knowable through a necessarily false representation, a Manichean division that threatens to reproduce the static, essentialist categories it seeks to undo. In the same way, the doctrine of multiculturalism encourages different groups to reify their individual and different identities at their most different, thus . . . encouraging extremist groups, who become 'representative' because they have the most clearly discernibly different identity. It is only recently that cultural critics have begun to develop accounts of the commerce between cultures that map and shadow the complexities of its generative and destructive processes. Historically,

however, comparatively little attention has been given to the mechanics of the intricate processes of cultural contact, intrusion, fusion and disjunction" (5).

6. I am arguing against Ato Sekyi-Oto's *Fanon's Dialectic of Experience*, which describes Fanon's dialectic as akin to the poststructuralist dissemination of binary hierarchies. I will argue that Fanon doubles quite systematically the Hegelian dialectic, only to attempt to dismantle it at the end of the chapter "Concerning Violence" in a less systematic way.

7. See Hussein Abdilahi Bulhan's *Frantz Fanon and the Psychology of Oppression*.

8. Gendzier's *Frantz Fanon* explains in depth Fanon's Marxist leanings.

9. As Hegel states in *The Philosophy of History*, "According to this abstract definition it may be said of Universal History that it is the exhibition of Spirit in the process of working out the knowledge of that which it is potentially. And as the germ bears in itself the whole nature of the tree, and the taste and form of its fruits, so do the first traces of Spirit virtually contain the whole of that History" (17–18).

10. For more recent ontological models that envision reciprocity and social parity, see Hwa Yol Jung's *The Crisis of Political Understanding: A Phenomenological Perspective in the Conduct of Political Inquiry* and Maxine Sheets-Johnstone's *The Roots of Thinking*.

11. I will use the masculine singular "he" when referring to the settler and the native as does Fanon.

12. We can therefore state that the racial categories produced by colonial discourse emerge in a dialectical relation where only the Western subject functions as a primary or "positive term." That is, only the Western subject acquires a specific cultural definition by rejecting the qualities of its non-Western "Others."

13. Said makes a similar argument in *Culture and Imperialism*.

14. Bhabha frequently points out the potential instability of hybrid identity. He uses the term hybridity to indicate the textual moments where colonial discourse subverts its own authority. More specifically, in "The Commitment to Theory" (*New Formations*, 5 [1988, 5–23], the term hybridity describes moments of counter-authority that dismantle various binary hierarchies between Self and Other constructed along the lines of race, class, or gender. Bhabha refers to "the 'hybrid' moment of political change," stating: "Here the transformational value of change lies in the re-articulation, or translation, of elements that are *neither the One* (unitary working class) *nor the Other* (the politics of gender) but something else besides which contests the terms and territories of both" (13).

15. For biographical information on the intellectual currents that influenced Fanon, see Irene Gendzier's *Frantz Fanon: A Critical Study*.

CHAPTER SEVEN

The Problem of Cultural Relativism: Said's *Orientalism* and *The World, the Text, and the Critic*

Given that the problem of cultural relativism has become central to the field of ethics, it is not surprising that Edward Said's *Orientalism*[1] is regarded as one of the most significant interventions in the ethical debates of cultural and literary studies. While contributing to contemporary ethical thought, however, Said deliberately avoids offering the kind of systematic normative models that characterize philosophical discourse. As is the case with his intellectual precursor Michel Foucault, Said's ethical inclinations become discernible in his choice of topic rather than the set of prescriptions he offers as an alternative to Orientalism. Said is particularly interested in exposing the manner in which Western discourses have depicted non-Western cultures as inferior in order to dominate them. At the conclusion of *Orientalism*, Said raises a crucial question, one that is also explicitly articulated by his critics: "Is this book an argument only *against* something, and not *for* something positive?" (326). This essay will explore this question along with other commonly raised objections to *Orientalism*. In addressing critical responses to Said's work, we will also examine how the ethical and epistemological lines of inquiry pursued by *Orientalism* and refined by *The World, the Text, and the Critic*[2] have furthered understanding of the problem of cultural relativism. While *Orientalism* only touches upon the problem of how cultures could represent each other less distortedly, *The World, The Text, and the Critic* attempts to offer a solution to this problem by proposing that the figure of the wordly intellectual functions as a critic of and mediator among cultures.

In *Orientalism*, Said describes representation as an intersection between ethics and epistemology. He analyzes not only how one represents given subjects, but also the normative assumptions that motivate those representations. "My analysis of the Orientalist text," Said announces, "places emphasis on the evidence, which is by no means invisible, for such representations as representations, not as 'natural' depictions of the Orient" (21). Said's critique of Orientalist discourse raises a number of more general questions that interweave epistemological, ethical, and political concerns: "How does one *represent* other cultures? What is *another* culture? Is the notion of a distinct culture (or race, or religion, or civilization) a useful one, or does it always get involved either in self-congratulation (when one discusses one's own) or hostility and aggression (when one discusses the 'other')? ... How do ideas acquire authority, 'normality,' and even the status of 'natural' truth?" (326). Clearly, for Said, ethical questions—such as, how should cultures treat each other?—are bound inextricably to epistemological questions—such as, how can societies represent each other in a truthful, fair, and respectful manner? Because the author frames ethical problems in epistemological terms, most of the normative critiques leveled against Said's work have to do, appropriately, with epistemology. Critics maintain that Said represents Orientalist discourses as a dialectical relation between Orient and Occident that does not capture the complexity, historical variation, and internal contradictions of Western discourses and cultures.

The purpose of this essay is to critique two representative critiques of Said's work—presented by Denis Porter and Aijaz Ahmad—in order to trace the development from a single dialectical to a double dialectical model of culture in Said's work. Both Porter and Ahmad, I will illustrate, maintain that Said's *Orientalism* presents the cultural interaction between Orient and Occident in terms of what I will call a "single dialectical" process. In a "single dialectical" relation, the Orient is defined solely as the non-Western: that is to say, as a negation of the Occident. In such a description, the Orient has no positive identity of its own acquired, in turn, by means of the negation of Occidental characteristics. A single dialectical process indicates, for example, that the West becomes rational only as it differentiates itself from representations of an irrational non-Western world; that it becomes the paradigm of culture by distinguishing itself from uncivilized societies.[3]

While examining the validity of Porter's and Ahmad's critiques of Said's supposedly single dialectical depiction of Orientalism, this essay also identifies the textual moments that point to a way beyond such binary and hierarchical distinctions between Western and non-Western societies. I plan to show that Said's more nuanced depictions of Orientalist discourse observe a double dialectical process. In a double dialectics, the West defines itself by distinguishing itself from its cultural Others and, reciprocally, non-Western cultures also define themselves by negating Western qualities. When we understand the formation as a double dialectical process, we acknowledge that both Orient and Occident are hybrid cultures whose identities are determined by a process of mutual incorporation and differentiation.

It may be obvious from this brief exposition that this essay is only partly concerned with Said's work and principally concerned with elaborating the transition from a single to a double dialectical model of cultural interaction. At the same time, Said's work is central to my project. In defending Said against two of his critics, I aim to show that he is one of the most important contemporary scholars who reflects upon the limitations of representing the relation between Orient and Occident in terms of a binary opposition. On the one hand, *Orientalism* illustrates systematically how Orientalist discourse relies upon a single dialectical process to set up the Orient as the negation of Occidental civilization. On the other hand, Said's work resists describing the Orient only as a lack of Western culture, showing points of resistance and doubling within Orientalist discourse. In so doing, Said begins to elaborate a double dialectical model of culture. Such a model of cultural interaction, I would argue, is more appropriate for our postcolonial world. Postcolonial societies today define themselves through a more complex series of juxtapositions and comparisons rather than solely in terms of the hierarchical opposition between Orient and Occident.

Furthermore, by beginning to outline a double dialectical relationship among (post)colonial societies, Said's work also enables readers to imagine a path beyond two false universalisms: a generalized ethnocentrism that is blind to its own biases and an empty abstract humanism that assumes the sameness of all societies.[4] That is, when he represents cultural relations as a double dialectical process, Said moves away from a one-sided discourse of victimization while nevertheless justifiably criticizing cultural domination. The author hopes that once societies realize that, as a result of their dialectical entanglement, they cannot purify themselves of their "Others," they will find strategies of peaceful coexistence. In the conclusion of *Orientalism*, Said gestures, like Fanon, toward dismantling the dialectic itself. Insofar as both single and double dialectics describe a process whereby cultures acquire value only by negating the value of other cultures, they have only a limited use in establishing respect among different societies.

Said consequently also envisions a world that is no longer ruled by hierarchical oppositions. He arrives at a cultural model that overcomes the twin discourses of oppression and victimization. Once we accept the undeniable fact that throughout history most societies have engaged in brutal power struggles and conquests, Said implies, we can pursue one of two paths. On the one hand, we can adopt cultural relativism and argue that if no society is perfect, then all societies should be beyond criticism since no society has the moral authority to judge another. On the other hand, starting from the same premise that no society is morally perfect, we can also conclude that all societies should criticize themselves and one another since they may be better equipped to see each other's flaws. A process of mutual critique, this second argument goes, may improve the world. I believe that Said's work, particularly the elaboration of "critical consciousness" as a mediation among cultures in *The World, the Text, and the Critic*, leads to an ethics of intercultural critique. Critical consciousness combines cultural partiality with the open-minded universalist commitment to forge more respectful relations among different societies. To see how Said's work makes the transition from a single to a double dialectical understanding of culture, let us now turn to his critics, particularly to those who charge that his theoretical model remains trapped in a single dialectical logic that juxtaposes oversimplified representations of Western and non-Western worlds.

Is Reality the Opposite of Representation?

A first set of charges, most emphatically voiced by Denis Porter, asserts that Said's *Orientalism* is, above all, epistemologically confused. According to Porter, most of the ethical problems we encounter in Said's work stem from the fact that the author cannot make up his mind about what the Orient is and how accurately it can be depicted. On the one hand, Said argues that representation is by definition distorted and ideological. On the other hand, he calls for cultural representations that are truthful and fair. Said's very project, Porter maintains, epitomizes this internal contradiction. While exposing the distortion and bias of all representation—particularly of French and English representations of the Middle East and North Africa—Said assumes the validity of his own characterization of Orientalist discourse, arguing:

From his introduction on, Said vacillates over the opposition between truth and ideology. On the one hand, he reaches the conclusion that there is no distinction between pure and political knowledge. (2) He even claims that "all cultures impose corrections upon raw reality, changing it from free-floating objects into units of knowledge" (67). On the other hand, in a discussion of representation he seems to imply, if only negatively, that a form of truth is obtainable; he comments for example that "what is commonly circulated is not truth but representations" (21), that there is perhaps a 'real' and consequently knowable Orient.[5]

I believe that Porter's objection is valid only if Said, indeed, presents the relation between truth and ideology as a single dialectic. For this is precisely the process that Porter describes when he frames the problem of representation as an either/or: either there is a possibility of absolute truth, or all knowledge is equally false. In this epistemology, falsehood functions as the negation of truth. That is, Porter's objection implies that Said regards truth as the elimination of every distortion and bias until a given representation emerges clear and objective. Once Porter assumes that Said's epistemological framework operates according to the logic of the single dialectic, Porter concludes that "the contradiction is never fully resolved in Said's book in part because he deals in such problematic concepts as 'raw reality' and 'the material itself' without reference to an epistemology that legitimates them" (180).

The question, however, remains: When Said claims that the information circulated about the place and fiction called "the Orient" is "not truth but representations," does he necessarily oppose the transparency of reality to the obscurity and falsehood of representation? Said, himself, denies this contrast. He claims that, although not based on "fact," Orientalist discourse itself is not only a form of representation, but also a material reality that has actual cultural effects. Representations are real in the sense that they affect people's beliefs and behavior. Said explains: "This evidence [of Orientalism] is found just as prominently in the so-called truthful text (histories, philosophical analyses, political treatises) as in the avowedly artistic (i.e., openly imaginative) text" (21). Orientalism can be understood as a phenomenon that permeates all aspects of society and culture. Being a literary scholar who analyzes narrative strategies rather than an historian who verifies the veracity of documents, however, Said maintains that "The things to look at are style, figures of speech, setting, narrative devices, historical and social circumstances, not the correctness of the representation nor its fidelity to some great original" (21). Said's description of his method reflects more than his literary training. It also

CHAPTER SEVEN

expresses his philosophical belief that there is no raw reality that is accessible to human beings without the mediation of representation.

Porter's objection implies that Said presents the question of truth and error not only as a single dialectical relation—where, as noted, error is defined as non-truth—but also as an opposition between epistemology and ontology. According to Porter's reading, either all forms of knowledge and communication are distorted or, in his own words, "there is perhaps a 'real' and consequently knowable Orient" (21). Is it fair to say, however, that these two statements contradict each other? I believe that, logically, Said can state that there is a real world that has been distortedly represented as the Orient *and* that other kinds of representations could capture it better or more accurately than Orientalist discourse.

To assess the validity of Porter's epistemological critique, let us explore further the following questions: Is Said framing the related problematics of truth versus falsehood and of reality versus representation as a single dialectical opposition? Or is he allowing for a more nuanced understanding of representation, whereby all truth conveyed by human beings is indeed a form of representation, but some representations are superior to, or more accurate than, others? If Said's work indicates the latter possibility, then how does his epistemology permit critics to differentiate between degrees of truth and error? To begin addressing these questions, I should state that I do not believe that Said ever implies that there is no geographical reality called "the Orient." Nor is he arguing, as Porter indicates, that this geographical reality yields its own self-evident truths, which have been distorted by Orientalist representations. In other words, I maintain that ontology for Said is not the opposite of epistemology. Rather, like Foucault, Said argues that, from an anthropocentric perspective, being and knowledge are interrelated. To understand the relation between reality and representation assumed by Said's work, let us examine briefly Foucault's concept of discourse, which underpins Said's study of Orientalism.

By the time Said published *Orientalism*, Foucault had developed the concept of discourse. This concept represented the relation between language and reality in a different manner than that conceived by traditional humanistic scholarship. Said did not need to rehearse Foucault's exposition of discourse. He only had to indicate that Foucault's concept served as an epistemological foundation for his argument:

> I have found it useful here to employ Michel Foucault's notion of a discourse, as described by him in *The Archaeology of Knowledge* and *Discipline and Punish*,

to identify Orientalism. My contention is that without examining Orientalism as a discourse one cannot possibly understand the enormously systematic discipline by which European culture was able to manage—and even produce—the Orient politically, sociologically, militarily, ideologically, scientifically, and imaginatively during the post-Enlightenment period. (2–3)

According to Said, the term "Orientalism" refers to Western texts and practices that aim to master non-Western cultures. Such texts and practices do not necessarily share common rules or strategies. They do, however, interweave a narrative about the "Orient" that represent it as simultaneously exotic—meaning feminine, desirable, and ready for conquest—and barbaric—meaning as cultures in need of Western civilization. For Said, as for Foucault, discourse figures as an all-encompassing term. It refers both to textuality (such as written or oral statements that produce "the Orient" as an object of Western knowledge) and to a series of practices and institutions (such as the academia or colonialist military ventures) that contributed to Western imperialism. Orientalism likewise includes several interrelated practices. First, it refers to the academic tradition of studying the Orient. Second, Orientalism is "a style of thought based upon an ontological and epistemological distinction between 'the Orient' and (most of the time) the Occident" (2). Third, the term also has a broader connotation, which encompasses all of the above meanings. According to Said, Orientalism signifies "the corporate institution for dealing with the Orient . . . by making statements about it, authorizing views of it, describing it, teaching it, settling it, ruling over it: in short, Orientalism as a Western style for dominating, restructuring, and having authority over the Orient" (3).

From this description, we can gather that Orientalism is a form of representation that promotes cultural imperialism. Does this mean that there is no such thing as a real Orient? Said answers: yes and no. On the one hand, the geopolitical entity called the Orient exists and is different from its distorted Orientalist descriptions. "The value, efficacy, strength, apparent veracity of a written statement about the Orient therefore relies very little . . . on the Orient as such," Said maintains. "On the contrary," he continues, "the written statement is a presence to the reader by virtue of having excluded, displaced, made superogatory any such 'real' thing as 'the Orient'" (21). On the other hand, over the centuries, the Orient has been historically saturated with the discourse of Orientalism. In Said's estimation, to think of an Orient that is free of Orientalist representations is to engage in a purely speculative exercise.

CHAPTER SEVEN

"In brief," Said summarizes, "because of Orientalism the Orient was not (and is not) a free subject of thought and action. This is not to say that Orientalism unilaterally determines what can be said about the Orient, but that it is the whole network of interests inevitably brought to bear on (and therefore always involved in) any occasion when that peculiar entity 'the Orient' is in question" (3). So far Said has described Orientalism only in epistemological and political terms: that is, as a series of competing discourses about the entity called the Orient, some of which (namely Orientalist ones) have had a greater effect than others (namely native ones) during the colonial period. Ontology, or the reality of the land and peoples themselves, has entered the picture only negatively: as something that cannot be known outside of its representations. Consequently, the discourse which acquires the highest historical influence is not the one that corresponds most closely to a reality called the Orient, but the reality deployed by the stronger power. "The Orient was Orientalized," Said adds, "not only because it was discovered to be 'Oriental' in all those ways considered commonplace by an average nineteenth-century European, but also because it *could be*—that is, submitted to being—*made* Oriental" (6).

To account for the tenacity of Orientalist discourse, Said couples Foucault's proposition that truth is a function of power with Antonio Gramsci's concept of "hegemony":

> One ought never to assume that the structure of Orientalism is nothing more than a structure of lies or of myths which, were the truth about them to be told, would simply blow away.... It is hegemony, or rather the result of cultural hegemony at work, that gives Orientalism the durability and strength I have been speaking of so far. (5–6)

A hegemonic discourse represents the ideology of the dominant class. By means of force and persuasion, this ideology gains cultural currency and eventually acquires the status of truth itself. Said maintains that, as opposed to myth, which is often assumed to be fictive, Orientalist discourse was accepted as factual. Orientalist representations sedimented over time to constitute part of the history of the location and peoples they claimed to depict. Once he describes the Orient in terms of a series of contradictory discourses, however, Said appears to posit, as his critics maintain, that the Orient has no ontological status whatsoever; that it is just a set of ideas proposed by different groups with different cultural and political interests. This is not the case, however. Said emphasizes that "it would be wrong to conclude that the Orient was essentially an idea, or a creation with no corresponding reality. . . . There were—and are—cultures and nations whose location is in the East, and their lives, histories, and customs have a brute reality obviously greater than anything that could be said about them in the West" (5).

The Orient and the Occident, the critic acknowledges, are real geopolitical entities. Their reality, however, is apprehended by humans only through language:

> [I]s not merely there, just as the Occident itself is not just there either. We have to take seriously Vico's great observation that men make their own history, that what they can know is what they have made and extend it to geography: as both geographical and cultural entities—to say nothing of historical entities—such locales, regions, geographical sectors as "Orient" and "Occident" are man-made. . . . [The Orient and the Occident] thus support and to an extent reflect each other. (5)

Said proposes that the Orient and the Occident exist in a specific linguistic relation: namely, a binary hierarchy that presents "the idea of European identity as a superior one in comparison with all the non-European peoples and cultures" (7). To understand better the connection established by Said between the reality of the Orient and Orientalist representations of it, let us examine the aspects of Foucauldian epistemology, and more generally, the poststructuralist understanding of reference, that underpins Said's argument.

Following Ferdinand de Saussure's linguistics,[6] poststructuralist scholarship regards "language" as a system of signs that are defined *diacritically*, or in a negative relation to one another. For example, the word "man" acquires meaning when contrasted to other words that either resemble it phonetically and graphically (such as "tan" or "van") or conceptually (such as "woman"). In turn, the two ways in which we have described the resemblances among words—as either graphic/phonetic or conceptual—corresponds to Saussure's distinction between the *signifier* (or the sound/image) and the *signified* (or the conventionally assigned meaning or concept) that comprises a sign. The relation between the signifier and the signified is arbitrary. It is not motivated by some intrinsic feature of the signifier, signified, or their relation. Instead, it differs from language to language and is established by convention.

This formulation of the sign both envelops and brackets the referent, or the "real" object to which the sign refers. It envelops it because it renders impossible any unmediated or naturalized understanding of the relation between a word and the object or concept it names. Although language does not correspond to pure reality, our perception and comprehension of the material world is made possible only by linguistic systems. Furthermore, systems of signification are not only imperfect—since they do not provide us with access to things-in-themselves—but, as Derrida illustrates, also unstable. In an effort to grasp the "essence" of given referents—such as "the Orient"—we move from one inadequate approximation to another—such as the imperfect synonyms "the Middle East" or "the Far East." This potentially endless chain of signification, poststructuralists claim, is restricted only by contextually-specific communicative conventions. Because the material world is, as far as human beings are concerned, enveloped in systems of signification, it too becomes understood as a sign. In this sense, language refers not only to words, but also to all the systems of signification that designate concepts, images, things, and geopolitical areas such as the Orient.

By using an inclusive concept of language, poststructuralist critics such as Foucault and Derrida are able to counter the frequent charges that they are setting up a "prison house of language" that ignores the material world and reduces meaning to destabilizing plays of signification. For example, in his response to John Searle's critique, Derrida clarifies that,

> What I call "text" implies all the structures called "real," "economic," "historical," socio-institutional, in short all possible referents. Another way of recalling that "there is nothing outside the text." That does not mean that all referents are denied [. . .] [b]ut it does mean that [. . .] one cannot refer to this "real" except in an interpretive experience.[7]

As for Derrida, so for Foucault and Said, "discourse" means more than verbal statements. It refers to the historical processes, institutions, and practices whereby truth and knowledge assume given material configurations. To explore the nature of that materiality, however, we need to consider the epistemologist Roy Bhaskar's intervention in contemporary debates about the relation between things and words, or between reality and representation.[8]

Bhaskar argues that poststructuralist conceptualizations of the interaction between discourse and the material world are uncritically one-directional. He acknowledges that poststructuralist theories, such as Foucault's, provide sophisticated accounts of the ways in which social codes, norms, practices, or discourses shape the material world. But what about the ways in which the material world partly determines social constructs? What of the ways, for example, in which the geopolitical reality called the Orient delimited what could be said about it by Orientalism or any other type of discourse? Bhaskar argues that the latter question, though perhaps as important as the former, is either conflated into the first (by antipositivist poststructuralist criticism) or inadequately answered by reductive versions of naturalism (by positivist scholarship). Along with other sympathetic critics of poststructuralist theory, Bhaskar hints that this blind spot has to do with the Saussurean bracketing of the referent. Or, as he phrases it, it results from an insufficient theorization of ontology.

To understand why poststructuralist scholarship brackets the referent, we must return to the structuralist definition of the sign. In poststructuralist theory, the referent does not disappear. Instead, it becomes disconnected. The focus of analysis shifts from ontological speculation about what an object or concept may be "in itself" to the epistemological investigation of the ways in which it is registered, interpreted, and modified by human beings. The usefulness of Bhaskar's criticism is that it complements the question "what does the material world look and act like" with the question "how does the material world partly determine our constructions of it."

Although we will only be able to answer both questions anthropocentrically and relativistically, the second question is not exclusively anthropocentric. Bhaskar argues that, logically, epistemological and ontological issues must remain distinct:

> Unless knowledges and their objects possessed relatively distinct beings and histories, scientific change would be impossible and ontic change could not be reported. For to change, e.g. to correct or revise (as to substantiate and confirm) a description, the previously designated object must still be (adequately) susceptible to reference; and to refer to a change in an object (as to attest its stasis), its former descriptions must still be (sufficiently) available.... The heterogeneity of thought and things is thus a condition of change (and stability) in both domains alike. (*Scientific Realism*, 54)

Bhaskar's discussion of the relation between reality and knowledge leads us to reconsider the poststructuralist bracketing of the referent.

CHAPTER SEVEN

As mentioned, Bhaskar posits that the material world contributes to and delimits human perception and representation. In so doing, he does not attempt, as do positivists, to determine the boundaries between the natural or any kind of "real" world and our conceptions of it. As Bhaskar clearly admits, the two are epistemologically intertwined. Nevertheless, they are also distinct.

Said relies upon an epistemology that is similar to Bhaskar's. Said has often denied the fact that he is a poststructuralist partly because, I believe, his understanding of reference is closer to Bhaskar's than to Foucault's. Although *Orientalism* precedes Bhaskar's theories, his work, like Bhaskar's, clearly assumes that ontology influences epistemology, not only vice versa. Bhaskar's realist critique of the poststructuralist understanding of reference, a critique that is only implicit in Said's work, enables us to see that Said is not necessarily contradicting himself, as Porter claims, in arguing that there is a real geopolitical area that has been called the Orient *and* that we can represent this reality with varying degrees of accuracy. Only because of the close interrelation between ontology and epistemology are we able to recognize, for example, the statement that the Orient is a frozen wasteland as clearly false. Said's work implies that the Western discourses which represented the Orient in such a way as to dominate it were similarly false. Just as we cannot plausibly call the Orient a frozen wasteland, so we cannot call it primitive, uncivilized, or eager for colonization.

Thus, on the one hand, the geopolitical reality of the Orient enables us to differentiate between true and false—or at least plausible and implausible—descriptions of the Orient. On the other hand, both kinds of descriptions are, of course, expressed through language and shaped by the context in which they are produced. How can we describe theoretically this relation between ontology and epistemology? I believe that rather than being a single dialectic where epistemology is the negative of ontology, Said, like Bhaskar, assumes that such a relation observes the logic of the double dialectic. Ontology, understood as the pure reality that we, as humans, cannot apprehend is the negation of representation. In turn, if we presume that we attain no knowledge that is unmediated by our human perception, it follows that epistemology is the negation of pure being. Both knowledge and being exist in this interdependent relation. Semantically and philosophically, there can be no knowledge without some conception, however distant, of the reality of being and, conversely, (for human beings) there can be no reality which is not already a form of knowledge. Because reality and knowledge are dialectically intertwined, Said can rightfully claim that the entity called "the Orient" exists; that Orientalist discourses make false claims about it, and that truer claims could be made about it. These propositions constitute, in fact, the key arguments of *Orientalism*.

Is Orientalism Unitary?

A second line of criticism against Said's *Orientalism* asserts that, despite his subtle textual analyses, Said groups together the long tradition of Western discourses about "the Orient" from classical to modern times under the unifying term "Orientalism" without examining their internal contradictions and points of resistance. In his controversial book *In Theory*,[9] Aijaz Ahmad levels one of the most incisive of such critiques. He proposes:

> But let us return to the three definitions, especially the intermediate one which defines Orientalism as "a style of thought based upon an ontological and epistemological distinction between 'the Orient' and (most of the time) 'the Occident.'" It is rather remarkable how constantly and comfortably Said speaks—not only in this particular sentence but throughout the book—of a Europe, or the West, as a self-identical, fixed being which has always had an essence and a project, an imagination and a will; and of the "Orient" as its object—textually, militarily, and so on. (*In Theory*, 183)

Just as Porter claims that Said represents the relation between truth and error as a single dialectic that culminates in self-contradiction, so Ahmad argues that Said represents the relation between the Occident and the Orient as a single dialectic that essentializes the Occident. According to Ahmad, the binary dichotomy between the West and its negation, the non-West, turns Said's *Orientalism* into, at best, a self-contradictory argument and, at worst, a hypocritical project. *Orientalism* produces a fiction called "the Occident" much as Orientalist discourse creates the "Orient." Ahmad maintains that "Said seems to posit, stable subject-object identities, as well as ontological and epistemological distinctions between the two" (183). If we assume this to be the case, then, Ahmad asks, "in what sense . . . is Said himself not an Orientalist—or, at least, as Sadek et Azm puts it, an Orientalist-in-reverse? Said quite justifiably accuses the 'Orientalist' of essentializing the Orient, but his own essentializing 'the West' is equally remarkable" (183). The question we will pursue is: Does Said, indeed, present, "the same 'Europe'—unified, self-identical, transhistorical, textual—which is always rehearsed for us in the sort of literary criticism which traces its own pedigree from Aristotle to T. S. Eliot?" Let us examine this question by looking at one of Said's most general claims about Orientalism:

> [A] very large mass of writers, among whom are poets, novelists, philosophers, political theorists, economists, and imperial administrators, have accepted the basic distinction between East and West as the starting point for elaborate theories, epics, novels, social descriptions, and political accounts concerning the Orient, its people, customs, "mind," destiny, and so on. This Orientalism can accommodate Aeschylus, say, and Victor Hugo, Dante and Karl Marx. (2–3)

By commenting upon the longevity of Western Orientalist discourses, Said is not claiming that the West itself has remained constant throughout its history. On the contrary, he demonstrates that the apparent unity of both the Orient and the Occident is an effect of Orientalist discourse itself. It is Orientalism, not Said, that establishes a binary hierarchy between the Orient and the Occident. Nor do Said's nuanced textual analyses indicate that Orientalist discourse assumes the same form throughout history and in every text, from Aeschylus to Hugo, and from Dante to Marx.

In fact, Said's genealogical method itself precludes representing the history of discourses as continuous. A genealogy, by definition, identifies historically significant moments of cultural transformation. No discontinuity, however, can be established without reference to that which remains constant. Said's work explores the interplay between narrative and cultural continuities and discontinuities in Orientalist discourses. "My contention," Said explains, "is that without examining Orientalism as a discourse one cannot possibly understand the enormous systematic discipline by which European culture was able to manage . . . the Orient . . . during the post-Enlightenment period" (3). While the audience, historical context, medium of expression, and relationship established between the Orient and the Occident certainly differ among Orientalist discourses, such discourses share a common strategy: "In a quite constant way, Orientalism depends for its strategy on this flexible positional superiority, which puts the Westerner in a whole series of possible relationships with the Orient without ever losing the upper hand" (7). Despite their significant differences, Said concludes, Orientalist discourses consistently establish a binary opposition between the Orient and the Occident in which the Occident is presented as superior.

Is Orientalism a One-Sided Discourse of Victimization?

In addressing the issue of whether Said Occidentalizes the Occident, we have touched upon the third type of criticism that portrays Said's representation of Orientalist discourse as a single dialectical process. Several critics, most notably, once again, Ahmad and Porter, maintain that Said's perspective is one-sided. By presenting the Orient as the perpetual Other and victim of the Occident, Said fails to take into account the fact that Western cultures sometimes portray themselves as "the Others of their Others." He also fails to acknowledge that non-Western cultures, in turn, Occidentalize the Occident to serve their own political objectives. Porter asserts:

> [T]he feasibility of a textual dialogue between Western and non-Western cultures needs to be considered, a dialogue that would cause subject/object relations to alternate, so that we might read ourselves as the others of our others and replace the notion of a place of truth with that of a knowledge which is always relative and provisional. (181)

Porter suggests that once we attribute to other cultures characteristics that are very different, if not opposite from, our own, such cultures become essential to our self-definition.[10] Does this centralization of the peripheral lead to unsettling the logic of the single dialectic? Or does it merely invert the relation between binary terms without changing their hierarchical structure?[11] More specifically, expanding upon Porter's objection, we are led to ask: Does Said imply that the Occident consistently distorts the Orient and that, conversely, the Orient conveys the Occident in a truthful and apolitical manner? Or does he state that cultures engage in double dialectical relations and representations: that is, mutual distortions, points of resistance, as well as genuine efforts to understand and respect each other?

At issue here is not Said's choice to focus upon one particular problem—namely, Western (mis)representations of the Orient—but rather the ethical assumptions that support his critique. As we recall, Said is asking "how does one represent other cultures" in ways that are "not self-congratulatory to one's own culture or hostile and aggressive toward other cultures" (326). On the one hand, in posing this general question, Said obviously acknowledges that all cultures can, and indeed do, routinely produce essentialist discourses that aim to distort and master other cultures. On the other hand, it is equally obvious that the goal of *Orientalism* is to show only how Western discourses attempt to dominate the Orient, not how these strategies operate in reverse. We are therefore led to ask, is this ethical and scholarly bias legitimate?

Said addresses this question indirectly when he explains why his role is *not* to be an objective and comprehensive critic of all ethnocentric distortions. Adopting the Foucaultian premise that all critical perspectives are ideologically biased—especially those that proclaim objectivity—Said defends the political and ethical partiality that motivates his work. He explains that "The distinction between 'humanists' and persons whose work has policy implications, or political significance, can be broadened further by saying that the former's ideological color is a matter of incidental importance to politics—whereas the latter is woven directly into his material—indeed, economics, politics, and sociology in the modern academy are ideological sciences—and therefore taken for granted as being political" (9). Yet one of the goals of *Orientalism* is to illustrate that humanist discourse can be equally, if less overtly, political. Class, gender, and personal motivations "continue to bear on [what the intellectual] does professionally, even though naturally enough his research and his fruits to attempt to reach a level of relative freedom from the inhibitions and the restrictions of brute, everyday reality" (10).

It is not that the scholar has no burden of proof or standards of accuracy, Said qualifies. Scholarly criteria, however, do not eliminate, and are in fact partly determined by, historical, social, political, institutional, and personal biases and circumstances. "For there is such a thing as knowledge that is less rather than more, partial than the individual (with his entangling and distracting life circumstances) who produces it. Yet this knowledge is not automatically nonpolitical" (10). Said situates knowledge in relation to two social axes. He calls the first one *strategic location*, "which is a way of describing the author's position in a text with regard to the ... material he writes about" (20). He calls the second one *strategic formation*, "which is a way of analyzing the relationship between texts and the way in which groups of texts, types of texts, and even textual genres, acquire mass, density and referential power among themselves and thereafter in the culture at large" (20). These two concepts explain why all discourses are biased. They are not only influenced by a critic's personal circumstances and preferences, but also by the historical context in which they gain (or fail to gain) cultural currency.

Said's defense of contextual truth-claims made by inherently biased discourses raises another important question: What kinds of biases are justifiable and what kinds are not? More bluntly, what distinguishes the biases of Orientalist discourse from Said's admittedly partial critique of Orientalist discourse? To answer this question, we must return to the theoretical framework of *Orientalism*, and particularly to its elaboration of the relations between knowledge and power. Such relations are, once again, more explicitly presented by Foucault and his critics.

The Ethics of Partial Reading

Said is not the only genealogical scholar to be sharply criticized for his supposed ethical blind spots. Foucault, his precursor, has also been famously accused of normative confusion. Jürgen Habermas and Nancy Fraser maintain that Foucault offers inconsistent normative standards. His work contests some types of dominative power relations while arbitrarily elevating others. I will cite Fraser's objection to Foucault's ethical framework at some length because, in my estimation, it provides one of the most thorough and succinct critiques of the normative inconsistency, which may characterize genealogical scholarship:

> I have noted some indications that [Foucault's] description of modern power is in fact not normatively neutral.... I must also note that Foucault does not shrink from frequent uses of such terms as "domination," "subjugation," and "subjection" in describing the modern power/knowledge regime. [. . .] Foucault calls in no uncertain terms for resistance to domination. But why? [. . .] Only with the introduction of normative notions of some kind could Foucault begin to answer such questions.... Foucault fails to appreciate the degree to which the normative is embedded in and infused throughout the whole of language at every level and the degree to which, despite himself, his own critique has to make use of modes of description, interpretation, and judgment formed within the modern Western normative tradition.... Foucault is normatively confused.... Now, the fact that Foucault continues to speak . . . the language of humanism need not be held against him. Every good Derridean will allow that there is not, at least for the time being, any other language he could speak.... Foucault himself acknowledges that he

cannot simply discard at will the normative notions associated with the metaphysics of subjectivity.[12]

These charges, I believe, apply as much to Said's *Orientalism* as to Foucault's work. As noted, Fraser argues that Foucault's ethical bias is a result of normative confusion. She targets what she regards as Foucault's at times confused (that is, multiple and logically inconsistent) and at other times hidden or missing normative assumptions that are in part complicit with the humanist ethics he rejects. I will first consider the second part of Fraser's objection and then return to the first.

In the second part of her statement, Fraser points out that one cannot deduce that all power is equally (il)legitimate from the observation that all knowledge involves the exercise of *some* power relations. Hence Fraser, Habermas, and other sympathetic critics urge Foucault to delineate the criteria and processes that enable scholars to distinguish legitimate from illegitimate uses of power. Pursuing a similar line of argumentation to Fraser's, Habermas accuses Foucault of three interrelated substitutions: (1) instead of elucidating communicative and hermeneutic structures of meaning, Foucault analyzes "structures that are meaningless in themselves"; (2) instead of differentiating claims in terms of (non)validity, he is only interested in exploring these issues "as functions of power complexes"; and (3) he avoids the problems of truth and value and of their justification "in favor of value-free explanations."[13]

Foucault rejects the assumptions that underpin Habermas's and Fraser's criticisms. By arguing that the normative discourses of "truth," "right," and "value" have legitimated forms of domination, Foucault justifies his epistemological shift from what he calls "the traditional question of political philosophy [. . .] of how is the discourse of truth [. . .] able to fix limits to the rights of power," to the problem of "what rules of right are implemented by the relations of power in the production of discourses of truth."[14] In their genealogies, Foucault and Said move away from the traditional problematic of political philosophy that questions what constitutes legitimate or illegitimate power and who is responsible for its exercise. Turning this problematic on its head, Foucault and Said explore instead the political effects of various discursive processes that either legitimize or delegitimize power. Foucault engages in this metacritique of traditional political philosophy not because he finds normative distinctions between different ways of exercising power irrelevant. Rather, he does so because he considers the typology of legitimate versus illegitimate power problematic itself. According to Foucault, such a distinction must be established and deliberated within a given context or tradition and informed by local, competing, and often clashing ethical assumptions and political goals.

Let us now turn to the first part of Fraser's objection to Foucault, that faults him for not being normatively consistent. In light of our previous discussion, it becomes clear that Foucault engages in a critique of normative consistency. His alternative models of subjectivity, based upon those abjected as "other" by modern ethical discourse—including the insane, hermaphrodites, and hysterical women—underscore the fact that ethics that strive for consistency tend to be exclusionary and hierarchical. Said makes a similar claim when he argues that the assumption that knowledge produced in the contemporary West is (or should be) "nonpolitical, that is scholarly, academic, impartial, above partisan or small-minded doctrinal belief" is largely an illusion that protects, rather than exposes, scholarly bias. The debate between critical theory and genealogy over ethics illustrates that, as is the case with all cultural analyses that do not pose as all-knowing or aim at what Judith Butler calls "a certain epistemological imperialism which consists in the presupposition that any given writer might fully stand for and explain the complexities of contemporary power,"[15] Fraser's and Habermas's critiques of genealogy privilege some vectors of discrimination, exclusion, domination, or simply cultural interest over others. For instance, while Fraser is primarily interested in examining how universalist discourses justify gender and class-based subordination, Foucault is primarily interested in seeing how modern universalist discourses restrict and also generate bodily freedom and autonomy.

Making a similar objection to Habermas's critique of genealogy as an idealist method of reading, Ahmad faults Said's *Orientalism* for its supposed neglect of the role of historical variation and political struggle in transforming discourse. By focusing strictly on cultural documents, Ahmad maintains, Said's work ignores the ways in which real life, and particularly class and gender relations, complicate the binary hierarchy established by Orientalist discourses between the Orient and the Occident:[16]

> Cultural domination is doubtless a major aspect of imperialist domination as such, and "culture" is always, therefore, a major site of resistance, but cultural contradictions within the imperialized formations tend to be so very

> numerous—sometimes along class lines but also in cross-class configurations, as in the case of patriarchal cultural forms or the religious modes of social authorization—that the totality of indigenous culture can hardly be posited as a unified, transparent site of anti-imperialist resistance. (8)

According to Ahmad, even if we grant Said his claim that Orientalist discourses aim to dominate the Orient, the very acts of interpretation, communication, political action, and struggle would sever the single dialectical relations between West and non-West presented by Orientalist discourses. The important issue at stake in this objection, I believe, is not whether Said examines the influence of life upon discourse, but rather which aspects of life he privileges in his scholarship. Real life, for Ahmad, refers primarily to class relations. Ahmad argues that the dichotomy between the dominant West and the dominated Orient only obscures more complex relations of power, such as those between those who control the forces of production and the working classes.

In describing briefly the objections against Foucault's and Said's critical biases from the perspective of yet other critical angles, I do not intend to fault Fraser, Habermas, or Ahmad for having normative preferences or to absolve Foucault and Said of theirs. Instead, I wish to illustrate more generally that methods of writing and reading are unavoidably "partial" in several ways. First, as noted, critical projects are *biased*. They either overtly or covertly privilege certain ethical and ideological concerns that are apparent not only in the critics' selection of texts and topics, but also in their methodological choices.

Second, critical projects target a limited rather than a universal audience (i.e., a reified "humanity") or a pluralist readership (i.e., everyone). As situated texts, they interpolate implied and real audiences that are at least partially informed about and sympathetic to their topic, objective, and methodology. As Ellen Rooney observes in her systematic critique of "pluralism," defined as "an ensemble of discursive practices constituted and bounded by a problematic of general persuasion," writing practices are based upon often unacknowledged but always present gestures of exclusion.[17]

Rather than denying or attempting to hide textual partiality, Rooney argues, an "emphasis on the gesture of exclusion is based on a critical awareness that historically irreducible interests divide and define reading communities; that interests and reading are inextricably bound together. To recognize exclusion is to respect the limits and interests imposed on the very possibility of persuasion" (*Seductive Reasoning*, 5–6). Rooney's study illustrates that explicit gestures of exclusion may exhibit more respect for the significant social differences that divide reading communities than do universalizing narratives that hide or deny their partiality by means of ostensibly inclusive rhetorical strategies. Said's *Orientalism*, which does not focus upon how class and gender relations might affect Orientalist discourse and omits any mention of how the Orient also conquered and colonized parts of the Occident, much as Foucault's genealogy of sexuality, which largely ignores the effects of gender upon sex, clearly qualify as partial readings. This scholarly bias, especially if unacknowledged, invites valid critiques.

Although I have argued that the charges leveled by Fraser and Habermas against Foucault and by Porter and Ahmad against Said have more to do with the different questions these critics are interested in posing rather than with the indefensible flaws in Foucault's and Said's readings, I also believe that these questions illuminate the formerly unseen limitations of genealogical scholarship. It is legitimate, I would conclude, to present one ethical perspective, as Said does in *Orientalism*. At the same time, as Said himself points out, it is also important to acknowledge the biases and incompleteness of such a perspective.

When acknowledged, ethical and textual partiality can be regarded as an openness to other subjects or texts. A dialogue with other readings entails a discontinuous process of mutual enrichment and critique; of partially untraceable intertextual borrowing and exchanges; and of unexpected contacts, clashes, and shifts of positions. By way of contrast to self-proclaimed "apolitical" or "universalist" readings, partial readings acknowledge their political, normative, and epistemological biases and intertextual character. Such readings are therefore aware of their selective and sometimes unsuspected reliance upon a set of prior texts that render them marketable and legible to a specific audience. They also allow for future unanticipated exchanges with other texts that contest their articulated positions, in a manner similar to Fraser's selective appropriation and critique of Foucault's theories of sexuality or Ahmad's reformulation of *Orientalism* to produce Marxist postcolonial scholarship.

Said, for one, calls for criticisms of his work that expand the scope of his project, precisely for the kind of readings his scholarship, because of its originality *and* its limitations, has spawned.[18] He states, "Perhaps the most important task of all would be to undertake studies in contemporary alternatives to Orientalism, to ask how one can study other cultures and peoples from a libertarian, or nonrepressive and nonmanipulative perspective" (24). Although such an ethics of intercultural dialogue is everywhere implied in *Orientalism*, it is nowhere to be found in this text. Said in fact acknowledges that his work has not fully overcome the single dialectical structure between Orient and Occident which it criticized in Orientalist discourse:

> But what I should like also to have contributed here is a better understanding of the way cultural domination has operated. If this stimulates a new kind of dealing with the Orient, indeed, if it eliminates the "Orient" and "Occident" altogether, then we shall have advanced a little in the process of what Raymond Williams has called the "unlearning" of "inherent dominative mode."

A first step in unlearning the "inherent dominative mode," I believe, consists of acknowledging that many societies, not just Western ones, wish to dominate other societies. For this reason, as Porter and Ahmad indicate, it is important to look at the obverse side of Orientalism. What might be called the reversibility of blame—or, more generally, the responsibility of all cultures toward other cultures—constitutes, as Said foresaw, one of the most important problems of our times.

Robert Young reiterates Said's call for the displacement of the binary hierarchy between Occident and Orient, arguing that this sense of responsibility involves a change in the representation of the relations between Self and Other, or between Us and Them: "The real difficulty has always been to find an alternative to the Hegelian dialectic—difficult because strictly speaking it is impossible, insofar as the operation of the dialectic already includes its negation" (*White Mythologies*, 6). I have called such an alternative logic a double dialectics, a process whereby cultures mutually externalize features that they associate with other cultures to define their own identities. Eventually, however, cultures need to move beyond such reciprocal negations. As Said indicates in the more optimistic moments of his texts, only an operation which dismantles the dialectic itself can produce cultural representations that are less distorted by ideology.

Before attempting to identify such an operation, however, we must first return to an earlier epistemological problem: If Said assumes that not all representations are equally distorted by ideology, then how does he depict the relations between politics and ethics? Given his criticism of Orientalism and search for alternative modes of representation, it is clear that Said regards the domains of politics and ethics as both interrelated and separate. In fact, his argument depends upon this very distinction. Were he to assume that every cultural interaction necessarily translates into hierarchical power relations, he could not justify his appeal that Western cultures abandon their prerogatives. Why would the West abandon its political advantage without, that is, accepting some generalizable standards of justice? In the conclusion of *Orientalism*, Said envisions a way for knowledge to work more fairly in the service of power: "Perhaps if we remember that the study of human experience usually has an ethical, to say nothing of a political, consequence in either the best or worst sense, we will not be indifferent to what we do as scholars. And what better norm for the scholar than human freedom and knowledge?" (327). Said's appeal to human freedom and knowledge resonates with humanist discourse. Nonetheless, the universalist ideals such as freedom, equality, and knowledge cannot automatically include, as if by a simple process of addition, those whom it formerly excluded. As we recall, the equality of some was produced by means of the exclusion of a category of humans who were deemed inferior. Modern humanist concepts, therefore, must be used with caution. They are inherently double-edged swords.

We cannot displace the dichotomy between Orient and Occident by denying its existence and influence. As Said indicates, "there is no avoiding the fact that even if we disregard the Orientalist distinctions between 'them' and 'us', a powerful series of political and ultimately ideological realities inform scholarship today. No one can escape dealing with, if not the East/West division, then the North/South one, the have/have-not one, the imperialist/anti-imperialist one, the white/colored one" (327). The first step in displacing such binary oppositions, according to Said, consists of identifying them: "We cannot get around them all by pretending they do not exist; on the contrary, contemporary Orientalism teaches us a great deal about the intellectual dishonesty of dissembling on that score" (327). It is the intellectual's responsibility, then, to begin the cultural work that undoes the effects of Orientalism. The intellectual must engage in a sensitive criticism that balances an ethical integrity that could be called universalist with personal biases that could be called relativist.

Beyond the Dialectic:
The World, the Text, and the Critic

In *The World, the Text, and the Critic*, Said offers some possible answers to the main question raised by *Orientalism*: namely, how can cultures both judge and respect each other? He finds a mediating path between ethnocentrism and cultural relativism, I would argue, by plausibly introducing a form of universalist ethics into a relativist framework. This new universalist position follows from rather than contradicting his earlier questioning of ethnocentric universalism. In *Orientalism*, Said demonstrated that Orientalists, and in fact ideological dogmatists in general, present a false universal. They take culturally particular claims and argue that these beliefs should apply to all societies. By way of contrast, cultural relativists declare that all cultural practices are equally (in)valid. There are no universal ethical standards according to which to judge human conduct. As discussed earlier, Said cannot be a true cultural relativist since, at the very least, he condemns discourses that aim at domination. At the same time, as we have also seen, in *Orientalism* he explicitly avoids developing generalizable ethical justifications for that condemnation. In *The World, the Text, and the Critic*, however, Said develops such a broader normative framework by proposing the figure of the cosmopolitan intellectual as a means of critiquing both universalism and cultural relativism. The intellectual becomes what I call a double dialectical figure: one that negates both universalism and relativism to arrive at an ethical paradigm that transcends both extremes.

Said begins by arguing against descriptions of the intellectual as a solitary figure who rejects his cultural context. He states, for example, that "Benda is surely wrong, on the other hand, to ascribe so much social power to the solitary intellectual whose authority, according to Benda, comes from his individual voice and from his opposition to organized collective passions" (15). The intellectual, like any other person, is immersed in a cultural context that influences his interests and opinions. This does not mean, however, that he cannot distance himself from that culture. As Said continues to state, the intellectual, by

> going against the surrounding environment as well as allied to contesting classes, movements, and values, is an isolated voice out of place but very much of that place, standing consciously against the prevailing orthodoxy and very much for a professedly universal or humane set of values, which has provided significant local resistance to the hegemony of culture.... (15)

While embracing particularist values—that is, the values of his society—the cosmopolitan intellectual has, at the same time, a broad vision that enables him to avoid cultural chauvinism. He rejects essentialist models of cultural identity that automatically declare one group of people or society superior to all others. In fact, Said claims, such extreme partiality can only obscure critical consciousness:

> It has been the historical fate of such collective sentiments as "my country right or wrong" and "we are whites and therefore belong to a higher race than blacks" and "European or Islamic or Hindu culture is superior to all others" to coarsen and brutalize the individual consciousness. (15)

Although he may prefer his own culture, the intellectual acknowledges, at least in theory, the value of other practices and beliefs. Both the chauvinist and the intellectual dialectically combine relativist and universalist assumptions. They follow, however, inverse processes. The chauvinist begins with the negation of the category of universalism by arguing that the particular values of his culture are most valid. In the next move of his argument, however, the chauvinist negates cultural particularism by universalizing the values of his own society in declaring it superior to all others. The cosmopolitan intellectual follows a similar dialectical process: one that leads, however, to a different and more logically consistent ethical vision. He begins by rejecting universalism in acknowledging his cultural preferences. "On the one hand, the individual mind registers and is very much aware of the collective whole, context, or situation in which it finds itself," states Said (15). Unlike the chauvinist, however, the intellectual also rejects particularism. He realizes that partiality for one's culture must be moderated by a critical distance toward one's cultural values and a respect for other societies. Said summarizes this double movement of the critical consciousness:

> On the other hand, precisely because of this awareness—a worldly self-situating, a sensitive response to the dominant culture—that the individual consciousness is not naturally and easily a mere child of the culture, but a historical and social actor in it. And because of that perspective, which introduces circumstance and distinction where there had only been conformity and belonging, there is distance, or what we might also call criticism. (15)

Said's explanation of the ethical role of the intellectual covers two of the blind spots of *Orientalism*. It not only offers a normative paradigm, but also develops the concept of agency, which had been described as an anonymous network of discourses in the earlier work. As the agent of a new ethical vision that begins to overcome the impasse between relativism and universalism, the intellectual functions as a mediating figure among cultures. His critical consciousness enables him to be both insider and outsider to his own society. As Said explains, the intellectual is neither completely detached from the values of his culture nor so immersed in that culture that he cannot see its flaws. Thus, Said elaborates, "the critical consciousness is a part of its actual social world and of the literal body that the consciousness inhabits, not by any means an escape from either one or the other" (15–16).

Phrased differently, the intellectual reaches a balance between what Said calls "filiation," or regarding one's own cultural values as second-nature, and "affiliation," or engaging in a distancing social critique. According to Said, the truly critical consciousness overcomes both complete identification with and complete rejection of his culture. To understand this sublation, let us return to Said's definition of the key terms "filiation" and "affiliation":

> Thus if a filial relationship was held together by natural bonds and natural forms of authority—involving obedience, fear, love, respect, and instinctual conflict—the new affiliative relationship changes these bonds into what seem to be transpersonal forms—such as guild consciousness, consensus, collegiality, professional respect, class, and the hegemony of a dominant culture. The filiative scheme belongs to the realms of nature and of "life," whereas affiliation belongs exclusively to culture and society. (18–19)

The new ethical agency that Said calls "critical consciousness" must reject the unconditional loyalty that characterizes familial relations. The loss of such closeness to one's own heritage, Said argues, which has been regarded as "The loss of the subject, . . . is in various ways the loss as well of the procreative, generational urge authorizing filiative relationships" (20). At the same time, as noted, Said also negates the notion of the intellectual as a detached critical consciousness that is not affected by his own society. After negating filiation, the intellectual proceeds to negate affiliation. The result of this double dialectical process, Said explains, constitutes "the three-part pattern I have been describing—and with it the process of filiation and affiliation as they have been depicted" (20). While filial bonds may describe a naturalized perspective of culture, affiliation, "can easily become a system of thought no less orthodox and dominant than culture itself" (20). The figure of the intellectual represents an ethical agency that both incorporates and negates naturalized social values as well as the network of practices and institutions deemed most valuable to his society.

By pursuing this double dialectical process, Said's work offers a model of cultural difference that encourages societies to engage in mutual criticism from a perspective that is neither one of blind ethnocentrism nor one of starry-eyed relativism. Such a perspective inherits the double dialectical Enlightenment tradition that mediates between universalist and particularist claims about human ethics and knowledge. This dialectical process, I have argued throughout this book, contributes to a timely philosophy of common sense that acknowledges our limits while maintaining hope in human possibilities.

Notes

1. See Edward Said's *Orientalism*.
2. See Edward Said's *The World, the Text, and the Critic*.
3. As David Theo Goldberg observes in *Racist Culture: Philosophy and the Politics of Meaning*, during the eighteenth and nineteenth centuries, "primitive societies were theorized in binary differentiation from a civilized order: nomadic rather than settled; sexually promiscuous, polygamous, and communal in family and property relations rather than monogamous, nuclear and committed to private property—illogical in mentality and practicing magic rather than rational and scientific" (155).
4. In *On Human Diversity: Nationalism, Racism and Exoticism in French Thought*, Tzvetan Todorov usefully distinguishes between a clearly ethnocentric universalism and a potentially less ethnocentric one: "The only difference—but it is a crucial difference—is that the ethnocentrist takes the path of least resistance and proceeds uncritically: he believes that his values are the only values there are, and he is satisfied with this belief; he never really attempts to prove it. On the other hand, the nonethnocentric universalist (we might at least try to imagine such a creature) would try to find a rational basis for the fact that she prefers certain values to others; she would even be particularly vigilant with respect to those aspects of her own tradition that struck her as universal, and she would be prepared to abandon what was familiar to her in favor of a solution observed in a foreign country or arrived at by deduction" (2).
5. *The Politics of Theory: Proceedings of the Essex Conference on the Sociology of Literature*, ed. Barker et al., "Orientalism and its Problems" (Colchester: University of Essex, 1982), 179–80.

CHAPTER SEVEN

6. See Ferdinand de Saussure's *Course in General Linguistics*.

7. See Jacques Derrida's *Limited Inc*.

8. For Roy Bhaskar's elaboration of scientific realism, see *Scientific Realism and Human Emancipation* and *Reclaiming Reality: A Critical Introduction to Contemporary Philosophy*.

9. Aijaz Ahmad, *In Theory: Classes, Nations, Literatures* (London: Verso, 1992).

10. See Jacques Derrida's analysis of the aporia between the primacy of nature versus that of civilization in *Of Grammatology*.

11. Exploring this question in *White Mythologies: Writing History and the West*, Robert J. C. Young discusses the pervasiveness of what I call "single dialectical" thought: "[I]f there is a politics to what has become known as post-structuralism, then it is articulated in this passage which unnervingly weaves capitalist-economic exploitation, racism, colonialism, sexism, together with, perhaps unexpectedly, 'History' and the structure of the Hegelian dialectic. . . . Not that Hegel himself is responsible. Rather, Cixous argues, unfortunately Hegel wasn't inventing things. The entire Hegelian machinery simply lays down the operation of a system already in place, already operating in everyday life" (1–4).

12. Fraser, *Unruly Practices: Power, Discourse and Gender in Contemporary Social Theory*, 30–55.

13. Habermas, "Some Questions Concerning the Theory of Power: Foucault Again," *Critique and Power*, ed. Michael Kelly (Cambridge: MIT Press, 1994), 87–88.

14. Foucault, the first lecture of "Two Lectures," Jan. 14, 1976, from *Critique and Power*.

15. Butler, *Bodies that Matter, On the Discursive Limits of Sex*, 19.

16. For a more complete analysis of Ahmad's objections to *Orientalism* see Nivedita Menon's "Orientalism and After," *Public Culture: Bulletin of the Project for Transnational Cultural Studies*, (Fall 1993): 65–76.

17. Rooney, *Seductive Reasoning*, 2.

18. I am thinking in particular of Lisa Lowe's *Critical Terrains: French and British Orientalisms*, a work that uses Said's insights to explore how gender interacts with race, ethnicity, and class in Orientalist discourse.

Bibliography

Ahmad, Aijaz. *In Theory: Classes, Nations, Literatures.* London: Verso, 1992.
Allison, Henry. *Kant's Transcendental Idealism: An Interpretation and Defense.* New Haven: Yale University Press, 1983.
Anderson, Wilda. *Diderot's Dream.* Baltimore: Johns Hopkins University Press, 1990.
Aquila, Richard E. *Matter in Mind: A Study of Kant's Transcendental Deduction.* Bloomington: Indiana University Press, 1989.
Barker et al., ed. "*Orientalism* and Its Problems." *The Politics of Theory: Proceedings of the Essex Conference on the Sociology of Literature* (Colchester, U.K.: University of Essex, 1982).
Beiser, Frederick C. *The Fate of Reason: German Philosophy from Kant to Fichte.* Cambridge Mass.: Harvard University Press, 1987.
Bernstein, Richard. *Beyond Objectivism and Relativism: Science, Hermeneutics and Praxis.* Philadelphia: University of Pennsylvania Press, 1983.
———. *The New Constellation: The Ethical-Political Horizons of Modernity/Postmodernity.* Boston: MIT Press, 1993.
Bhabha, Homi. "The Commitment to Theory." *New Formations* 5 (1988): 5–23.
Bhaskar, Roy. *Reclaiming Reality: A Critical Introduction to Contemporary Philosophy.* London: Verso, 1989.
———. *Scientific Realism and Human Emancipation.* London: Verso, 1986.
Bird, Graham. *Kant's Theory of Knowledge: An Outline of One Central Argument in The Critique of Pure Reason.* New York: Humanities, 1962.
Blum, Carol. *Diderot: The Virtue of a Philosopher.* New York: Viking, 1974.
Brewer, Daniel. *The Discourse of Enlightenment in Eighteenth-Century France: Diderot and the Art of Philosophizing.* Cambridge, U.K.: Cambridge University Press, 1993.
Bulhan, Hussein A. *Frantz Fanon and the Psychology of Oppression.* New York: Plenum, 1985.

BIBLIOGRAPHY

Butler, Judith. *Bodies That Matter: On the Discursive Limits of Sex.* New York: Routledge, 1993.
Cassirer, H. W. *Kant's First Critique: An Appraisal of the Permanent Significance of Kant's* Critique of Pure Reason. London: Allen and Unwin, 1954.
Caute, David. *Frantz Fanon.* London: Fontana, 1970.
Chateaubriand, René de. *Atala.* Paris: Gallimard, 1971.
———. *Génie du christianisme.* Paris: Stéréotype d'Herhan, 1807.
———. *René.* Geneva: Droz, 1970.
Chinard, Gilbert. *L'exotisme américain dans l'oeuvre de Chateaubriand.* Geneva: Slatkine Reprints, 1970.
Collins, Arthur W. *Possible Experience: Understanding Kant's* Critique of Pure Reason. Berkeley: University of California Press, 1999.
Creech, James. *Diderot: Thresholds of Representation.* Columbus: Ohio State University Press, 1986.
Crocker, Lester G. *Diderot's Chaotic Order: Approach to Synthesis.* Princeton: Princeton University Press, 1974.
Derrida, Jacques. *Of Grammatology,* tr. Gayatri Chakravorty Spivak. Baltimore: Johns Hopkins University Press, 1976.
———. *Limited Inc.* Evanston, Ill.: Northwestern University Press, 1988.
Descartes, René. *Discourse on Method,* tr. Donald Cress. New York: Hackett, 1980.
Diderot, Denis. *Supplément au Voyage de Bougainville.* Paris: Garnier-Flammarion, 1972.
Diderot, Denis, and Jean Le Rond d'Alembert, eds. *Encyclopédie, ou Dictionnaire Raisonné des Sciences, des Arts et des Métiers.* Stuttgart: Friedrich Frommann Verlag, reprinted 1966.
Fanon, Frantz. *The Wretched of the Earth,* tr. Constance Farrington. New York: Grove, 1965.
Findlay, J. N. *Kant and the Transcendental Object: A Hermeneutic Study.* Oxford: Oxford University Press, 1981.
Foucault, Michel. *The Order of Things,* tr. A. Sheridan. New York: Random House, 1970.
Fraser, Nancy. *Unruly Practices: Power, Discourse and Gender in Contemporary Social Theory.* Minneapolis: University of Minnesota Press, 1989.
Geismar, Peter. *Fanon.* New York: Dial, 1971.
Gendzier, Irene. *Frantz Fanon: A Critical Study.* New York: Pantheon, 1973.
Goldberg, David Theo. *Racist Culture: Philosophy and the Politics of Meaning.* Oxford: Blackwell, 1993.
Good, James, and Irving Velody, eds. *The Politics of Postmodernity.* Cambridge, U.K.: Cambridge University Press, 1998.
Goodman, Dena. *Criticism in Action: Enlightenment Experiments in Political Writing.* Ithaca: Cornell University Press, 1989.

Guyer, Paul. *Kant and the Claims of Knowledge*. Cambridge, U.K.: Cambridge University Press, 1987.

Guyer, Paul, ed. *Introduction to The Cambridge Companion to Kant*. Cambridge, U.K.: Cambridge University Press, 1992.

Habermas, Jürgen. *The Theory of Communicative Action*, tr. Thomas McCarthy. 2 vols. Boston: Beacon, 1989.

Hegel, Georg Wilhelm Friedrich. *The Philosophy of History*, tr. J. Sibree. New York: Wiley, 1944.

Hume, David. *Enquiries Concerning Human Understanding and Concerning the Principles of Morals*. Oxford: Oxford University Press, 1972.

Irigaray, Luce. *An Ethics of Sexual Difference*, tr. Carolyn Burke and Gillian Gill. Ithaca: Cornell University Press, 1984.

Jordanova, Ludmilla. *Sexual Visions: Images of Gender in Science and Medicine between the Eighteenth and Twentieth Centuries*. Madison: University of Wisconsin Press, 1989.

Jung, Hwa Yol. *The Crisis of Political Understanding: A Phenomenological Perspective in the Conduct of Political Inquiry*. Pittsburgh: Duquesne University Press, 1979.

Kant, Immanuel. *Critique of Pure Reason*, tr. Norman Kemp Smith. New York: Macmillan, 1972.

———. *Prolegomena to any Future Metaphysic*, tr. Paul Carus. Indianapolis: Hackett, 1977.

Kelly, Michael, ed. *Critique and Power*. Cambridge, Mass.: MIT Press, 1994.

Lowe, Lisa. *Critical Terrains: French and British Orientalisms*. Ithaca: Cornell University Press, 1991.

Lynes, Carlos. *Chateaubriand as a Critic of French Literature*. Baltimore: Johns Hopkins University Press, 1946.

Lyotard, Jean-François. *The Differend: Phrases in Dispute*, tr. Georges Van Den Abbeele. Minneapolis: University of Minnesota Press, 1988.

———. *The Postmodern Condition: A Report on Knowledge*, tr. Geoff Bennington and Brian Massumi. Minneapolis: University of Minnesota Press, 1993.

McDonald, Christie V. *Dialogue of Writing: Essays in Eighteenth-Century French Literature*. Waterloo, Ontario: Wilfrid Laurier University Press, 1984.

Menon, Nivedita. "*Orientalism* and After." *Public Culture: Bulletin of the Project for Transnational Cultural Studies* (Fall 1993): 65–76.

Moscovici, Claudia. "Beyond the Particular and the Universal: D'Alembert's 'Discours préliminaire' to the *Encyclopédie*." *Eighteenth-Century Studies*. Vol. 33, no. 3 (2000): 383–400.

———. *Gender and Citizenship: The Dialectics of Subject-Citizenship in Nineteenth-Century French Literature and Culture*. Lanham, Md.: Rowman & Littlefield, 2000.

———. "Hybridity and Ethics in Chateaubriand's *Atala*." *Nineteenth-Century French Studies* (Fall 2000).

———. *Perusals into (Post) Modern Thought*. Lanham, Md.: University Press of America, 2000.
Nicholson, Linda, ed. *Feminism/Postmodernism*. New York: Routledge, 1990.
Norris, Christopher. *Reclaiming Truth: Contribution to a Critique of Cultural Relativism*. Durham, N.C.: Duke University Press, 1996.
———. *The Truth about Postmodernism*. Oxford: Blackwell, 1993.
O'Neal, John C. *The Authority of Experience: Sensationist Theory in the French Enlightenment*. University Park: Pennsylvania State University Press, 1996.
O'Neill, Onora. *Constructions of Reason: Explorations of Kant's Practical Philosophy*. Cambridge, U.K.: Cambridge University Press, 1989.
Perinham, Marie. *Holy Violence: The Revolutionary Thought of Frantz Fanon, an Intellectual Biography*. Washington, D.C.: Three Continents, 1982.
Porter, Charles. *Chateaubriand: Composition, Imagination, and Poetry*. Saratoga, Calif.: Anma Libri, 1978.
Richard, Jean-Pierre. *Paysage de Chateaubriand*. Paris: Editions du Seuil, 1967.
Rooney, Ellen. *Seductive Reasoning*. Ithaca: Cornell University Press, 1989.
Rousseau, Jean-Jacques. *Discourse on the Origin of Inequality*, tr. Donald A. Cress. Indianapolis: Hackett, 1992.
Said, Edward. *Culture and Imperialism*. London: Chatto and Windus, 1993.
———. *Orientalism*. New York: Vintage, 1979.
———. *Orientalism: Western Representations of the Orient*. London: Routledge and Kegan Paul, 1978.
———. *The World, the Text, and the Critic*. Cambridge, Mass.: Harvard University Press, 1983.
Saint-Amand, Pierre. *Diderot: Le Labyrinthe de la Relation*. Paris: Librairie Philosophique J. Vrin, 1984.
———. *The Laws of Hostility: Politics, Violence, and the Enlightenment*. Minneapolis: University of Minnesota Press, 1996.
Sarup, Madan. *An Introductory Guide to Post-Structuralism and Postmodernism*. Athens: University of Georgia Press, 1993.
Saussure, Ferdinand de. *Course in General Linguistics*. London: Verso, 1978.
Schiebinger, Londa. *The Mind Has No Sex? Women in the Origins of Modern Science*. Cambridge, Mass.: Harvard University Press, 1989.
Schor, Naomi. *Bad Objects: Essays Popular and Unpopular*. Durham: Duke University Press, 1995.
Sekyi-Oto, Ato. *Fanon's Dialectic of Experience*. Cambridge, Mass.: Harvard University Press, 1996.
Selden, Raman. *A Reader's Guide to Contemporary Literary Theory*. Lexington: University of Kentucky Press, 1989.
Sheets-Johnstone, Maxine. *The Roots of Thinking*. Philadelphia: Temple University Press, 1990.
Shwyzer, Hubert. *The Unity of Understanding*. Oxford: Clarendon Press, 1990.

Switzer, Richard. *Chateaubriand*. New York: Twayne, 1971.

Todorov, Tsvetan. *On Human Diversity: Nationalism, Racism and Exoticism in French Thought*, tr. Catherine Porter. Cambridge, Mass.: Harvard University Press, 1993.

Van Cleeve, James. *Problems from Kant*. Oxford: Oxford University Press, 1999.

Woddis, Jack. *New Theories of Revolution: A Commentary on the Views of Frantz Fanon, Regis Debray and Herbert Marcuse*. New York: International, 1972.

Young, Robert. *Colonial Desire: Hybridity in Theory, Culture and Race*. New York: Routledge, 1995.

——. *White Mythologies: Writing History and the West*. New York: Routledge, 1990.

Index

affiliation, 154
Ahmad, Aijaz, 9, 130–31, 141, 143, 147–49, 150
Allison, Henry, 30, 49n3
American Indians. *See* Native American culture
amorphous intuition, 46
Anderson, Wilda, 83, 87–88, 90n6, 91n14
anthropocentric knowledge, 54, 64, 66
anthropocentric universalism, 65, 68
appearances, 41–42, 43–45
The Archaeology of Knowledge, 134–35
aristocratic societies, 77–89
arts and sciences, 63–64
Atala, 8, 93–108, 109nn6–7
Atala, 98, 104–6
Aubry, Père, 107
The Authority of Experience: Sensationist Theory in the French Enlightenment, 71n20

Bad Objects: Essays Popular and Unpopular, 111nn22–24
Berkeley, George, 1, 29, 38
Bernstein, Richard, 4–5
Bhabha, Homi, 110n13, 127n14
Bhaskar, Roy, 4, 138–40

Blum, Carol, 84
Brewer, Daniel, 56, 58–59, 65, 71n18, 72n25
Butler, Judith, 147

Cartesian philosophy, 56, 59–60, 62, 66, 71n12, 71n19
Cassirer, H. W., 30–31
the categories, 38–39, 42
causal reasoning, 29, 33, 34–35
Chactas, 98–107
Chambers, Ephraim, 59
Chateaubriand, François-René de, 8, 93–108, 109n6, 110n18
Chateaubriand, 110n18
Chateaubriand: Composition, Imagination, and Poetry, 112n26
Chateaubriand as a Critic of French literature, 111n19
chiasmus, 54, 55, 70n8
children, gender of, 86
Christianity, 105, 106–8, 111n24, 112nn26–28
civilization, development of, 108n2
civilized man, 93–94, 94, 101
Cixous, 156n11
class relations, 147–48, 149

163

INDEX

classification and order of *Encyclopédie*, 64, 72nn24–25
Collins, Arthur W., 30
Colonial Desire: Hybridity in Theory, Culture and Race, 94–95, 126n5
colonialism, 8–9, 82, 98, 99, 113, 114, 116–24
common sense, 3–4, 9, 27, 91n16
communication, 3–4, 52, 53, 85, 138
complexity, 57
compromise, 119–21
consciousness, 42, 153–55
consensus, 15–17
Creech, James, 57–58, 77
critical thought, 77, 90n5, 147
Criticism in Action, 77, 81, 90n5, 91n16
Critique of Pure Reason, 1–2, 5, 6–7, 29–49
Crocker, Lester G., 86
cross-cultural principles, 75
cultural imperialism, 135
cultural relativism, 7–8, 9, 75–76, 152
culture and cultures, 93, 94, 101; decolonialization and, 114–26; differences in, 76–89; diffusionist model of, 78–81; disillusionment of, 107, 112n25; domination by, 147–48; elements of, 107, 112n29; exchange of, 76, 77–80, 83, 85, 89, 90n6; exotic nature of, 80, 90n8; French, 76–89; hybridity of, 8, 94–95, 99, 110n13, 110n17, 118, 127n14; identity, 97, 115, 153; interaction between, 9, 130–31; nature and, 103–4; partiality for, 153; purity of, 97–98; representations of, 77, 143–44; savage cultures, 93; Spanish, 102–3; Tahitian, 76–89; understanding of, 149–50
custom, 1, 35–36, 40

d'Alembert, Jean Le Rond, 1, 5, 7, 51–73
decolonialization, 113–26

Derrida, Jacques, 138
Descartes, René, 29, 59–61, 71n19, 72nn21–23
dialectic, 51, 70n2
Dialogue of Writing: Essays in Eighteenth-Century French Literature, 57–58, 71n14
Diderot, Denis, 1, 7–8, 51, 59; *Diderot's Dream*, 71n9, 71n12, 90n6, 91n14;v *Supplément au Voyage de Bougainville*, 75–91
Diderot: Le Labyrinthe de la Relation, 57
Diderot: Thresholds of Representation, 57–58, 77
Diderot: The Virtue of a Philosopher, 84
Diderot's Chaotic Order, 86
Diderot's Dream, 71n9, 71n12, 90n6, 91n14
The Differend, 6, 18–28
the differend, 20–21, 26
diffusionism, 78–81
Discipline and Punish, 134–35
Discours de la Méthode, 60, 72nn21–23
"Discours préliminaire," 5, 7
discourse: domination and, 152; humanist, 144; meaning of, 138; Orientalist, 134–35, 142, 143–45, 148; universalist, 147
The Discourse of Enlightenment, 58–59, 71n18, 72n25
Discourse on the Origin of Inequality, 108nn2–3, 109n5
dogmatic relativism, 36

empirical knowledge, 35–36
empirical observations, 34
empiricism: empiricist skepticism, 29, 32–36; idealism and, 37–38, 39; rationalism and, 59–62
empirico-transcendental doublet, 53
Encyclopédie, 56–60, 63–66, 69, 71n9, 71n14, 72nn24–25

Enlightenment, 2, 4–6; contrasted with postmodernism, 16; knowledge and, 15–16, 56–60, 63–66, 69, 71n9, 71n14; universalist logic and, 56–57
Enquiries Concerning Human Understanding and Concerning the Principles of Morals, 33
ethico-political norms, 5
ethics, 75, 147, 150–51; *Atala,* 93–108, 109nn6–7; cultural exchange, 76; depiction of Orient and, 132–33; the intellectual and, 152–53; law and, 20–21; Lyotard's approach to, 18–22; sexual behavior and, 87–89; women and, 83–84
ethnocentrism, 81, 131, 152, 155n4
European culture, 98, 100–102, 105–6, 112n29
exclusion, gesture of, 148–49
experiences, 40, 43, 46–48
exploratory voyages, 79–80
external reality, 37–38, 39
eyewitnesses to Holocaust, 24–25

Fanon, Frantz, 8–9, 113–26
Faurisson, Robert, 19–20
fecundity, 86–87
female allegory, 111n22
femininity, 111n23
Fénelon, François, 101, 111n19
filiation, 154
Foucault, Michel, 52–53, 59, 71n19, 129, 134–36, 138, 145–46
Frank, Anne, 22, 23, 27
Fraser, Nancy, 145–47, 149
fraternal patriarchy, 83, 85
French civilization, 100–102, 111n19
French culture, contrasted with Tahitian, 76–89

gender, 83–84, 86, 103–4, 105, 111n22, 147–48, 149

genealogical classification, 62–64, 142, 145–46, 147, 149
Génie du Christianisme, 107
God, 34, 44, 61–62, 72nn22–23, 106
Goldberg, David Theo, 109n10, 155n3
Golden Age, 108nn2–3
Goodman, Dena, 77, 81, 90n5, 91n16
Gramsci, Antonio, 136–37
Guyer, Paul, 49n8

Habermas, Jürgen, 3–4, 52–53, 145–47, 149
Hegel, Georg, 7n9, 156n11
hegemony, 136–37
heterogeneity, 3
historical process, 115
Holocaust, 14, 19, 21–28
humanism, 145
humanist discourse, 144
Hume, David, 1, 27, 29, 33–36
hybridity of cultures, 8, 94–95, 99, 110n13, 110n17, 118, 127n14

idealism, 29, 37–38, 39
idealist-subjectivist, 30
identity, 97, 12, 114–26, 126n5
ideology vs. truth, 133–34
imperialism, 147
In The Theory of Communicative Action, 3–4
In Theory, 141
information, 52, 68–69
the intellectual, 152–54
intercultural communication, 85
intercultural hierarchy, 8
internal experience, 39
Introduction to The Cambridge Companion to Kant, 49n8
Irigaray, Luce, 54, 70n8

judgment, 42

INDEX

Kant, Immanuel, 1–2, 5, 6–7, 29–49
"Kant Disfigured," 19
Kant's Transcendental Idealism, 30, 49n3
knowledge, 1–2, 13, 16, 34, 38; *a priori* concept and, 40–41; acquisition of, 29, 66; Brewer's views of, 58–59; d'Alembert's theory of, 54; Descartes's views of, 59–61, 72n21; *Encyclopédie,* 56–60, 63–66, 69, 71n9, 71n14; Foucault's theory of, 52–53; genealogical classification of, 62–64; Hume's views of, 33–36; Leibnitz's views of, 32–33; objective, 7, 51–52, 55; power and, 16–18; reality vs. perception, 31; social axes of, 144–45; sources of, 37; subjective, 55; theory of, 51; truth and, 31–32; unity of, 15–16; vs. reality, 139–40

labyrinth, 57
language: concept of, 137–38; language games, 13, 15, 17–18, 53
law of gravity, 35
law and legal systems, 20–21, 39
The Laws of Hostility: Politics, Violence, and the Enlightenment, 90n4
laws of nature, 35
legitimation of knowledge, 16, 17–18
Leibnitz, Gottfried, 32–33, 38–39
Lettres persanes, 77
lifeworld, 3–4
Lynes, Carlos, 111n19
Lyotard, Jean-François, 2–3, 5, 6; *The Differend,* 18–28; *The Postmodern Condition,* 13–18

manifolds, 41–47
Marxist dialectic, 120–21
materialism, 60, 62–63, 71n20
McDonald, Christie V., 57–58, 64, 71n14
metanarratives, 2

moderate skepticism, 36
modernism, definition, 15
monad, 33
monarchies, 110n15
Montesquieu, 77, 90n5
moral relativism, 7–8, 19–21
morality, 4, 7–8, 21, 49n8, 93–94
multiculturalism, 126n5
myth and magic, 122–23

Natchez culture, 102–3
Native American culture, 98, 100–101, 103–7, 112n29
native-settler strategies. *See* settler-native relationships
nature, 32, 33, 99–100; appearances and, 42; culture and, 103–4; Kant's view of, 38–39; laws of, 35, 38–39, 39–40, 41; morality and, 93; Tahitian culture and, 84–85
Nazi historians, 23–28
The New Constellation, 4–5
Newton, Isaac, 35
noble savage, 93–94
non-sense, 27–28
normative confusion, 146
normative consistency, 147
Norris, Christopher, 4, 19–20
noumena, 30, 38, 41, 49n3, 50n13

objective knowledge, 40, 55
objectivism, 29–30, 31, 32, 65; knowledge and, 52; negation of, 14, 42, 54; relativism and, 53–54; subjectivism and, 37–40
objects, concepts of, 37–38
Occident vs. Orient, 9, 99–100, 130–31, 137–38, 141–44, 150–51
On Human Diversity: Nationalism, Racism and Exoticism in French Thought, 90n8, 112n29, 155n4
O'Neal, John C., 71n20

The Order of Things, 52–53, 59
Orient vs. Occident, 9, 99–100, 130–31, 137–38, 141–44, 150–51
Orientalism, 9, 129–52
Orientalism, 135–36, 141
Orientalist discourse, 130–31, 133–34, 143–45, 148
Orou, 76, 83, 85–88

partiality, 148–49, 153
particularism, 54, 55, 62–69, 152–53
Patagonians, 79
Paysage de Chateaubriand, 110n17
perceptions, 31–32, 33–34, 37–39, 41, 66–68
personal experience, 22–23
The Philosophy of History, 127n9
physical evidence, Holocaust, 25–28
Plato, 25
pluralism, 148
political philosophy, 146–47
politics, 144, 150–51
Porter, Charles, 112n26
Porter, Denis, 9, 130–31, 132–34, 141, 143, 150
positive identity, 97
The Postmodern Condition, 2, 5, 6, 13–18
postmodernism, 2–3, 15–19
power, 52, 97, 145, 148; asymmetrical, 98; colonialism and, 119; decolonialization and, 116–17; knowledge and, 16–18, 151; truth and, 136–37; use of, 146–47
primitive societies, 80, 81, 94, 108n3, 109n10, 155n3
purity of culture, 97–98

racial categories, 95–98, 109n11, 111n22, 127n12
Racist Culture: Philosophy and the Politics of Meaning, 109n10, 155n3
rationalism, 29, 38, 59–63, 71n20
rationalist objectivist, 32–33, 39–40, 42

realist-objectivist, 30
reality, 26–27, 49n3, 139–40
reciprocal exclusion, 117
referent, bracketing of, 139–40
relativism, 61, 68; *The Differend* and, 20–21; negation of, 14, 27–28; objectivism and, 53–54; universalism and, 54–55, 69–70, 75–76, 154
René, 94, 111n20, 112n25
René, 101–2, 111n20
representations, 37, 43, 77, 132–41, 150–51
reproduction, 83, 86–87
republican civilization, 93, 109n4
Richard, Jean-Pierre, 110n17
Rooney, Ellen, 148
Rousseau Jean-Jacques, 93, 108nn2–5

Said, Edward, 9, 96–97, 129–55
Saint-Amand, Pierre, 57, 90n4
Saussure, Ferdinand de, 137, 139
savage cultures, 93, 101
Schor, Naomi, 111nn22–24
science, 49n8
scientific knowledge, 13
Searle, John, 138
self, 44
semiotic process, 5–6, 96, 97, 116
sensationism, 60, 71n20
sense perception. *See* perceptions
settler-native relationships, 116–19, 121–24
sexual behavior, 76, 83–89, 105–7
sexual differences, 83–84
sexuality, 86–87
shared experiences, 6
shared reality, 31
silence, Holocaust survivors, 25
skepticism, 32–33, 48
social inequality, 83–84
social structure, 87, 91n14
Spanish cultures, 102–3

strategic formation, 144–45
strategic location, 144
subjective knowledge, 55
subjective truth, 6
subjectivism, 29–30, 31, 32, 37–40, 42
subjectivist skepticism, 36, 39–40
sublation, 115
Supplément au Voyage de Bougainville, 7–8, 75–91
Switzer, Richard, 109n6, 110n15, 110n18, 112n25

Tahitians, contrasted with French culture, 76–89
technology, 17
The Theory of Communicative Action, 52
things-in-themselves, 138; experiences and, 46–47; Kant and, 30, 38, 41, 49n3, 50n13; manifolds and, 44–45; reality and, 29, 32
Todorov, Tsvetan, 81, 90n8, 112n29, 114, 155n4
transcendental idealism, 30, 32–36, 38–40
transsubjective communication, 52, 53
travel narratives, 77
Travels in America, 109n7
truth, 4, 17–18, 31; Descartes and, 61–62, 72n22; Habermas's definition of, 52; knowledge and, 31–32; power and, 136–37; truth-certainty, 29–30, 32, 60; truth-claims, 53, 58; truth-value, 15, 23; vs. ideology, 133–34

unity, 3
universal peace, 15
universal truth, search for, 17–18
universalism, 52, 65, 68, 152; *The Differend* and, 20–21; ethnocentric, 131, 155n4; form of, 75; negation of, 14, 18, 27–28; particularism and, 54, 55, 62–69, 153; rejection of by Descartes, 61; relativism and, 54–55, 69–70, 75–76, 154
universalist morality, 7–8
universalization, 56–57
utopic phase of decolonialization, 124–26

validity, 52, 61, 69
values, 83, 121–22, 152–55
Van Cleeve, James, 30
violence, 113–16, 124

White Mythologies: Writing History and the West, 156n11
Williams, Raymond, 150
women: ethics and, 83–84; Tahitian society, 83
world map, 57
The World, the Text, and the Critic, 129, 151–55
The Wretched of the Earth, 8–9, 113–26

Young, Robert, 94–97, 110n12, 126n5, 150, 156n11

About the Author

Claudia Moscovici teaches French literature and philosophy at Boston University. Her research focuses on explaining the development of democratic theories during the eighteenth and nineteenth centuries. In *From Sex Objects to Sexual Subjects* (Routledge, 1996), she examines the paradoxical fluidity and restrictions placed upon the notion of the individual in democratic societies, paying particular attention to gender roles. Through a comparison of eighteenth-century and contemporary political theory, she shows that the republican tension between regarding men and women as complimentary (along the lines provided by Rousseau) and regarding human nature as open-ended (along the lines provided by Diderot) continues to this very day in the way we experience our roles as democratic citizens. Her second book, *Gender and Citizenship* (Rowman & Littlefield, 2000), proposes a philosophical model—the double dialectic—to explain the development of women's significant roles as citizens in nineteenth-century French society. She is currently working on a book, entitled *Dystopic Utopias*, that examines the impasses and possibilities of democratic theory.